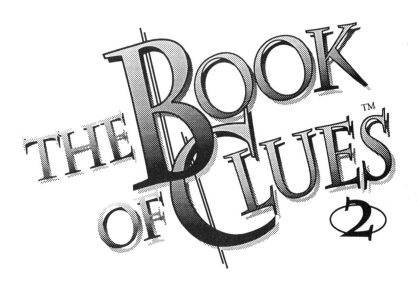

THE BOOK OF CLUES 2 ™

BY SHAY ADDAMS

QuestBusters™: The Book of Clues™ 2

Created and edited by Shay Addams

Solutions verified by Clancy Shaffer, Fred Philipp, Bruce and Peggy Wiley, and Russ Ceccola

Interior and cover design by Scott-Goodman Design

Interior layout by Schrock & Associates

Cover art by Bruce Jensen © 1994

ISBN   1-57280-004-6
Printed in the United States of America
0 9 8 7 6 5 4 3 2 1

DEDICATION

To Stephanie Alexis Cantero,

my darling granddaughter

Contents

Contents

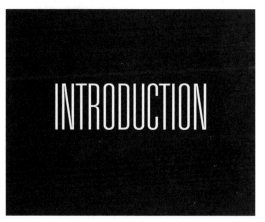

INTRODUCTION

BY
SHAY ADDAMS

Civilization's first recorded clue, which led to solving one of literature's earliest puzzles, was a simple ball of string. According to Greek mythology, Theseus unrolled the string to avoid getting lost in King Minos' labyrinth on Crete, where he sought to slay the Minotaur who dwelled at the center of the maze. The first English translation of the Greek myth about Theseus and the Minotaur referred to his ball of string as a "clew," and the word has been used since then to describe anything that leads to the solution of a puzzle.

Though the spelling has changed, we all still need an occasional clue to get through the multi-media mazes and defeat the monsters and Evil Wizards of today's adventure games. With this book in hand, you'll have no trouble opening that Mysterious Locked Door you suspect leads to the King's Treasure Room. (You may prefer to put the book down, however, while actually playing the game, as an independent research lab has established that pointing, clicking and interacting with adventure games can be conducted far more effectively when both hands are free.)

While it may seem like cheating to consult the *The Book of Clues* 2, or any other clue book or strategy guide, never think of this as a cheat book. Everyone cheats, especially the people who create adventure games. Instead, think of *The Book of Clues* 2 as your last line of defense in a world driven mad by megalomaniacal game designers who haven't a clue as to the meaning of the phrase "logical puzzle." Consider it your weapon of choice in the never-ending battle for truth, justice and the Zorkian way. Keep it under your pillow to swat mosquitoes in the middle of the night.

But do not sell it at the computer swap meet next Thursday. This book was printed with a special disappearing ink that is activated when placed within ten feet of a stack of 5.25" floppies, a table full of unlabeled chips and peripherals, and 50 computer maniacs milling about on a Sunday afternoon. You have been warned.

HOW TO USE THIS BOOK

To get the most out of this book, buy a stack of adventure games and play them night and day until hopelessly stuck. (If already stuck on a quest, skip to the next paragraph.) Then turn to the Table of Contents and look up the name of the quest you're currently stuck in. (If the solution is not in this book, please check the contents of the other books in the *QuestBusters* series: *Keys to the Kingdoms* and *The Book of Clues*.)

In the solution, scan the section headings to find the area of the game where you are stuck. Locate the answer, then get on with the quest. To make it easier to follow the often intricate steps of a solution, we have listed them line by line, rather than in conventional paragraphs.

The most important objects in every quest are listed in each solution's "Orbs & Stuff" table. The first column names the objects, and the name of the section that reveals its location is noted in the second column. The third column, "Also See Section(s)," refers you to every section of the solution that discusses the object, a sort of index to the walkthrough. If the object is discussed only in the section of the solution in which it is found, the third column will say "Location only." Treasure, equipment and other items not necessary for completing the game may be listed simply as "Various Armor" or "Assorted Weapons and Potions," for example.

Due to the near-universal implementation of auto-mapping, coupled with the relative ease of mapping today's adventures, few maps were deemed necessary. In addition to coordinates and specific directions, we have included maps only for the most maddening areas, such as those with teleports.

If the answer you find still doesn't work, review the preceding sections: sometimes you must have accomplished a prior feat before a subsequent solution will work, and some have their own peculiarities, which may be pointed out under the General heading at the top of the solution. (If nothing works, jot down the situation and teleport it to Clue Books Express, Dept Z, PO Box 85143, Tucson AZ 85754. along with a self-addressed, stamped envelope.)

AL-QADIM: THE GENIE'S CURSE

BY
CLANCY SHAFFER
& FRED PHILIPP

I N A WORLD DISTINGUISHED BY THE LOOK AND FEEL OF *THE ARABIAN NIGHTS*, AL-QADIM COMBINES REAL-TIME ARCADE-STYLE ACTION WITH CONVENTIONAL ROLE-PLAYING. IT IS A ONE-CHARACTER RPG IN WHICH YOU PLAY THE OLDEST SON OF THE AL-HAZRAD FAMILY. BLAMED FOR A CRIME THEY DIDN'T COMMIT, YOUR FAMILY HAS BEEN IMPRISONED BY THE RULER OF THE CITY OF ZARATAN, AND TO FREE THEM YOU MUST RESCUE THE CALIPH AND HIS DAUGHTER. BEHIND THE CRIME AND OTHER EVENTS IS THE GENIE'S CURSE, WHICH MAKES IT POSSIBLE FOR GENIES TO DISOBEY THEIR RULERS AND RUN AMOK.

GAMEPLAY CONSISTS MAINLY OF SEEKING OUT TREASURE, WEAPONS AND OBJECTS TO USE IN PUZZLE-SOLVING. MAGIC SPELLS AND POTIONS PLAY A MAJOR ROLE, ESPECIALLY IN THE COMBAT SEQUENCES. COMBAT TAKES PLACE IN AN AERIAL-VIEW DISPLAY, WHILE DUNGEONEERING IS CONDUCTED IN A 3D VIEW. MONSTERS AND THE PEOPLE YOU MEET APPEAR MUCH LARGER THAN IN MOST RPGS, AND

TYPE
Action Role-playing

SYSTEM
IBM PC & CD (Required: 386DX33+, 4 MB RAM, 256-color VGA, 100% Microsoft-compatible mouse, 15 MB hard disk. CD version requires MPC2-compliant double speed drive. Supports: Aria, Sound Blaster, Pro Audio, WaveBlaster, SoundScape, Sound Canvas)

COMPANY
Strategic Simulations

THE GRAPHICS ARE *AL-QADIM'S* STRONG POINT. IT LACKS FEATURES EXPECTED BY MOST MAZE-HOUNDS, THOUGH, SUCH AS AUTO-COMBAT AND AUTO-MAPPING. ULTIMATELY, *AL-QADIM* IS A DISAPPOINTMENT, AS THE MIXTURE OF OBJECT-ORIENTED PUZZLES AND REAL-TIME COMBAT NEVER QUITE GELS.

THE SOLUTION

GENERAL

The difficulty setting affects the monsters you will encounter, but not the puzzles.

THE MAZE

You will have to restart your maze journey if you lose your hit points or get caught by the curtain of energy that chases you through the maze.

Not far from the outset of your trip, look for three pressure plates.

Step on the left one, the middle one, and finally the right plate, which will lower the spikes for a short time.

Break one of the ceramic jars to get past.

At the pit, you must step on one plate at a time (this may be randomized, but right to left should work).

If you encounter three blocks of stone, use the left key to grab one and push it out of the way.

You will encounter three levers near ceramic jars: pull the center lever to fly over the jars.

Watch for traps until you get to the chest, then open it and get the loot.

Go north, and you will be teleported to your home city.

ZARATAN & THE BERRIES

(While in Zaratan, you can earn experience points by donating at the temple, helping a man repair his roof, and giving money to a beggar.)

Head north, where your sister will take you to your father.

Ask why he is worried, then talk to your Mother.

Help the Babazar family, who need purple berries from the Oasis.

Before leaving the city, visit your Aunt, who will have a present for you; use part of it to buy Healing potions at the store near the city gate.

Then visit your sister and get the magic sling.

Now leave the city and go west to get the berries, which are a little north of your starting point at the corner of the city.

A mermaid will appear and ask you to give a message to the Qadi.

Calling all Caliphs in Al-Qadim

·····················

THE TREATY

Return to the city, where your ex-Corsair trainer gives you a parchment with the words SALAB'LA JASUM ABA" — keep it!

Give the purple berries to Babazar, then go to the Quadi's Hall, where the Quadi want you to get a treaty signed between your family and the Wassabs.

Get your sister to sign by taking her to the Quadi house to meet with Wassab.

After the treaty has been signed, tell the Quadi about the message from the Mermaid and agree to return his message.

Return to the Oasis and tell the Mermaid, who will grant you access to the healing waters just west between two trees.

Look for a part of the water colored differently from the rest: this spot will completely heal you.

When you return to town and your father's Courtyard, you hear all the bad news and leave as soon as possible to search for the Princess.

You will find the Caliph along the northwest shore.

Take him back to town, where in the Quadi Court Yard you will find that your family has been arrested and you are forced to leave the city.

DEADMAN'S REEF

Find the Mermaid and tell her of your trouble, and she will tell you about a magic ship on Deadman's Reef and how to get there via turtle.

When you arrive, search the eastern side of the ship for chests hidden under bushes and get a small key and a large key.

Go to the west side, kill some ghouls and get a green key.

When you try to go aboard, use the sling to get rid of the archer.

On the ship, go into the hold, open the first door, kill the two ghouls, and then save the game.

Open the next door and slay the Wizard.

Get the Healing potion and Oil.

Go through the forward bulkhead (wall) and travel up to a circular, floating island.

Break the large globe, then use the small globe to heal yourself.

Return to the ship, talk to the Captain and learn the story.

Go to Bandar al-Sa'adat.

BANDAR AL-SA'ADAT

After reaching land via the small boat, walk due north to the Caliph's Palace, enter and talk to the Vizier.

Tell the Caliph you want to see your father and that he has nothing to fear from you; when asked if you know anything new about your family, say no.

Go west to the Dungeon entrance and use the third statement when answering the guard.

Pay the Dungeon fee, and the guard will take you to your father.

Tell your father about your adventures, ask how he is being treated and offer him a Healing potion.

Follow the hall across from your father's cell to visit your sister.

Find your mother by following the hall near your father's cell east as far as you can go, then south until it turns east and a little south.

Return to your father, who give you a Ring of Protection +1.

Exit the Dungeon.

Ask the Captain of the Guard to give your father a better cell.

He will do so for four hundred gold, but will usually settle for a little over 200 if you already spent some on potions.

Return to this town when your fighting ability increases later in the quest, and the Captain of the Guard will train you in new swordfighting moves.

SORCERER AL'MUTAN'S TOWER

Exit the city and go to the ship.

Sail home and visit the Sorcerer Al'Mutan in the Tower, just outside the northwest wall of the city.

Use the words from the Mermaid to enter "Azvllah Batan."

Inside, you are teleported to a dark area with the imprint of a face on the floor.

Step on the face and take the test.

Go west along the hall until you come to a gate with six spots on the floor in front of it.

Step on all six while they are lighted to open the gate: you must step on them all in order: 1, 2, 3, 4, 5, 6.

Continue west until you find a lever: pull it to get over the green scum on the floor.

The hall divides north and south: first pull the lever to the south, then the lever to the north.

Return south and stand on the face again.

Tell him who you are, then proceed north.

Pull the lever just in front of the wall of spikes, then go to the room in the south.

Just northeast of the face, walk through the moving wall.

Pull the lever inside and take the treasure.

Return to the face and go north.

Use the stones to cross the acid just to the north, then continue north until you reach a wall of moving spikes.

This is a timing puzzle: start in the lower left corner and slowly move across the spikes.

In the north, take the treasure and pull the lever.

Go south and take the eastern path until you reach a room full of circles.

15

ROOM OF CIRCLES

Step on the blue circle, and a new one will light up.

Continue stepping on each circle until all are lit, then pull the lever to the east.

Return to the hall where the two gold and green Jars are located.

Just to the north, enter the breathing wall.

Follow this hall until you see an arrow cut in the floor; it points east to a secret wall.

Inside, slay the poisonous spiders while keeping your distance.

Enter the secret wall and get the treasure, then return to the main hall.

Go to the face on the floor in the north and talk to it.

Pull the lever on the left, then the lever on the right and go north on the stones.

When the stones quit moving, you must kill the slime on the platform.

Talk with the face that appears, then go east.

MORE CIRCLES

Kill the bats and slime before proceeding to the six circles on the floor.

Step on the blue circle.

Another circle will turn blue; step on each until all circles are dark.

Step on the face and answer the questions as follows: 1) North 2) South 3) I do not know. Return to the central platform and go west.

THE SPIKES

Step on the face in the floor.

To get through the spikes, position the levers as follows, starting with the north: Left, Left, Right, Left, Right.

Always answer the woman's question with: " I would never do that."

Return to the central platform, and the face teleports you deeper into the dungeon.

Go carefully along the hall and kill the monsters one at a time until you reach a room with another pool of acid.

Step on the stones and go to the northwest corner.

Open the chest and get the treasure.

Continue to the southeast corner and open the chest.

Continue until you reach a lever.

Pull the lever, then seek out the central chest.

Leave this area by going south.

In the south, step on the next face and answer his question with: "He is a man without honor."

Continue west until you reach the tile puzzle.

THE TILE PUZZLE

Go to the north and pull the lever, then exit in the southwest corner.

On a 10 X 10 grid on graph paper, mark the locations that teleport you or turn blue.

You will see a pattern that will enable you to go south on the second line of tiles from the west side, but transfer to the western tiles about seven tiles down from the top. What happens is that you walk on each tile as it turns blue until you get to the northwest area, then you will be transferred to the southeast corner.

From the southeast corner, walk across the southern row of tiles to the two chests.

From the western chest, go north and west until you reach the top; then pull the lever, which sets up a new pattern.

Search for a pathway leading south on the second row from the west.

Go south, then take the first turn to the west.

Go west until teleported to another blue tile.

Go west and south to leave this area.

You will find another face in the floor: answer both questions with dialogue choice #1.

THE POOL OF ACID

Go through the walls of spears carefully to a large acid pool lined with stones.

Walk on the stones and pull each lever, and new stones will appear.

When you have pushed all the levers, go to the one just south of the entrance and pull it out, which opens a path to the south.

Continue pushing all the levers until you are taken to the east.

Speak with the next face in the hall and promise to never seek out the Mermaid.

Go north to the chest, then speak to the face in the Acid, who agrees to answer one question.

You will be teleported across the pool.

Go along the hall and up the stairway.

Follow the hall up another stairway and enter the door.

Talk with the Sorcerer and his wife and agree to get the Gilded Dove (buy it in Bandar).

Return to your ship and sail to the Isle of Shibaz.

THE ISLE OF SHIBAZ

When you arrive at the island, go directly east into the house.

Note the opening, then go south and get the scroll.

Go back north and east to a blocked doorway.

Move the stone and get the scroll along the north side.

Look for a book and memorize it.

Go east, then south, then east: you'll find another scroll just as you start east.

To the north, another scroll is behind a barrel (you need three scrolls before leaving this building).

Exit east from the building and enter the building directly ahead, which contains two chests.

Leave this building and go north.

When the furniture attacks you, destroy it one piece at a time by backing into the doorway; then take the loot.

You will encounter a lot of miniature Air Elementals; if low on Healing Potions, return to your ship to heal.

Go south from this building to a double line of torches.

Use Lightning or Sun spells on the two invisible ghouls.

Go around the south of this building to the western entrance, then east and north to three statues.

THREE STATUES

Feed the three scrolls to the statue on your right, then feed the one on the left a coin for each word.

Repeat the oath you memorized from the book and proceed north.

When you try to open the purple chest to the north, it will speak.

Use Answer 2 ("I intend to put Treasure in, not take it out.")

Then use Answer #4 and put in thirteen gems, which makes your sword more powerful.

Leave this building and go to the south-central area to find the Hermit.

THE HERMIT

Use Answer 2, then 3, then 1; the Hermit will invite you to see the library.

Go to the building just southeast of the torches and descend the steps.

Go north, east, north and west up through the arch and slay the four Great Ghouls.

THE SEALS

Go east out of the arch and past the statues to Seal #1.

Activate the Seal by stepping on it.

Take the first path north, then go east.

When you see the statue in the center of the corridor, go north and west to the lever.

Activate the lever, revealing Seal #2.

Step on the seal and quickly go west over the bridge, which may be burning.

Follow this road to an opening to the south.

Go south past the statues as far as possible; a spiked wall forms behind you.

Go east as far as possible, then south to the next intersection.

At the intersection, go west.

As you pass, ceramic jars and spiked walls appear.

Break the jars to proceed further west. (This will confirm you are on the correct road.)

Continue to Seal #3, then go west to where you started.

Go south to a maze of spikes around a lever, then work your way to the lever and the chest.

Seal #4 is slightly east and south — don't leave this area until you locate it.

Return to the bridge and proceed east.

Follow the path to a lever, pull it and cross the bridge.

Go south, pulling levers along the way until you reach a room full of jars.

Break them and get the booty.

Go west out of the jars room, past the line of statues, and go north as soon as possible.

Active Seal #5 and continue north to Seal #6 (both seals are an a little piece of land jutting west).

All seals are now activated, so go south to the south wall and then west to a chest surrounded by spikes.

Work your way around the spikes and get the treasure.

Now go west to the next area, then north to a magic portal with seals all around it.

THE MAGIC PORTAL

Activate only the center (lit) seal by walking over it to the north.

Go through the portal, then head east, then north to a lever.

The statues will interfere, but pull the lever and cross the skeleton bridge to get the flying rug.

The path on the west side leads to a book and seal.

Activate the seal, and you will see stairs leading down.

As soon as you reach the library, go east and take the first passage north, then take the first passage east.

In this passage you will encounter Rashidin.

After Rashidin exits, go south and west to a chest.

Put the mirror in the chest, which cause Jaza'ir Jiza Island to appear on the map.

Sail to Jaza'ir Jiza Island.

JAZA'IR JIZA ISLAND

There are four kinds of Genies in the Noble House: Efreet, Dao, Marid and Djinn.

Walk around the Wall of Fists to the south and through the Gateway of Fists.

Go through the gate to the north and continue until you meet an Efreet, who blocks the gate.

MULTIPLE PATHS

At this point, you can either complete four missions for the Efreet and get past her, or speak with the Dao to the east about the Singing Scimitar to get past. If you want to complete the four missions, skip to the next section, "The Efreet's Missions." If you prefer to speak with the Dao, which is faster, consult the following section, "The Singing Scimitar."

THE SINGING SCIMITAR

Go east of the Efreet and speak with the Dao about the Singing Scimitar.

20

Then go west and north of the Efreet to a small clearing.

Wait for Sha'ir to arrive on a flying carpet and land.

Talk to Sha'ir, and you'll learn more about the Singing Scimitar.

Return to the Dao, who says he'll help defeat the Efreet if you bring him the Scimitar.

Go back to the clearing and wait for Sha'ir to return, then talk to him and he'll tell you the Scimitar is on the Isle of Senat and where to find the Isle.

Go to the Isle of Senat.

Go east along the beach to an opening leading north.

There are three paths: take the north one, then the west fork at the next two junctions, and go northwest through the next intersection.

At the next fork, go southwest to a large gold chest.

Open the chest and take the Singing Scimitar and return to your ship.

Take the Scimitar back to the Dao, who will attack the Efreet.

While they are fighting, walk through the gate after she moves away from it.

Now skip down to the section called "The Chessboard."

THE EFREET'S MISSIONS

Speak with the Efreet, who will assign you four missions.

You can get the wisest snake in the world at the Reptilian Desire's in Main City.

After the Efreet claims it is not what it wants, walk away and return, and she will ask you to get the hottest coal in the world from the Katim.

Heating the coal quickly ruins it, so you walk away; return and talk to the Efreet again.

This time the Efreet wants a veil made by Idrind, which can also be bought in the Shop of Wonders in the city.

The Efreet burns the veil. Step away, then return, and she will demand the bottle of Emptiness.

ISLE OF SENAT

Go to the Travelers Rest in the City and talk to the Wise Man, Qutlum Ibn Tasheed, about the "Bottle of Emptiness."

He will tell you where to find the Isle of Senat.

On the Isle, save your game and hurry, because every minute here costs you hit points.

Go east along the beach to an opening leading north.

There are three paths: take the north one, then the west fork at the next two junctions, and go northwest through the next intersection.

At the next fork, go southwest to a large gold chest.

Open the chest and take the Vial (bottle) and return to your ship.

Return to the Isle of the Genie Lords and give the bottle to the Efreet.

When the Efreet claims there is something in the bottle, ask her to open it, swearing on your honor that it is empty.

When she opens it, she is sucked into the bottle and you can walk past her.

THE CHESSBOARD

As you go north, you find a giant chessboard.

There are four openings, each leading to a different Genie Lord.

Begin at the lower left corner and move directly forward until you have illuminated five squares.

Turn left until you have illuminated three more squares.

Turn left and light up one more square.

You will be transported to the Genie Lord who matches the color of the tiles you just illuminated (in this case, the two Genie Sister Lords).

Stay and talk with them, always using the correct name and checking the colors of their gowns.

Ask to leave them.

Take the northwest path to the Noble Emeret Domain.

Ask the Emerit about the Efreet, and listen until he completes his story.

Ask him to tell you about his Story Teller, Shahar I Zad.

Back at the Chessboard, use the northeast pathway and repeat the pattern described previously.

THE GENIE GEM

Ask the Noble Dao about the Shahar I Zade, and she says she has Shahar I Zade and will trade her for a Genie Gem.

Return to the Genie Sisters to inquire about a gem, answering questions about what you have learned from reading "Genies are different from Mortals."

They will ask you what you are willing to do for a Sky Gem.

Answer "Whatever they think is fair," and never change your answer.

They will give you a Gem and teleport you back to the Chessboard.

Give the Gem to Dao, who will give you Shahar I Zad.

Return her to the Noble Emeret, who will give you a potion that will help you against the fire of the Efreet Lord.

Now go to see the Efreet Lord Mirza Gubishbuskin, using the southwest entrance.

Walk through the massive flames in your path, and the Efreet Lord tells you about the Nameless Masters, explaining that your father was one and that he can tell you where to find him.

Return to the ship: you must now speak with your father.

THE CALIPH'S PALACE

After learning you can't see your father, leave the Palace.

On your way out, a man suggests that Chief Summa wanted to serve you a meal.

Go to the northeast section of the Palace and eat the meal.

Summa will send you to the Tariff Master near the city entrance to get a key for the Wine Cellar.

The Tariff Master sends you to the baker just south of the Palace and instructs you to ask for the Bone Key.

Do so, then return to Summa.

The key fits a door in the room east of Summa.

Go through this secret door and down the steps.

You must move stones to get through the doors to the west.

Read the note in the first cell and get the key from the southeast corner.

Proceed north, moving stones and fighting three Spiders.

In the north room, the wall to the east is a secret passage.

Go through the passage and open the third door on the north.

Agree to get the Cyclops out of town.

Disguise him and watch out for guards.

After passing Summa, put perfume on the Cyclops and save the game.

After the Cyclops is free, he give you a hint about the Island Hajar, which you might visit for the booty.

YOUR FATHER

Return to the Dungeon, read the scroll in the Cyclops' cell and put the stones on the large blocks to activate all six switches.

The main door will now open.

In the next hall, which runs south, push the bench and stone into their proper positions.

Go to the north wall and click on the lichen eight times.

Pull out the switch, and eight switches will appear.

Activate only the fourth switch from the north, and you can proceed further.

Enter the open cell and go south through a hole.

You can find a chest to the north, and another one to the northwest.

Return and go south, and you will see your father in a cell as you approach the secret entrance.

You must reach him without getting in front of any of Miniature Copper Automatons, which otherwise cannot see you.

Use empty cells and short halls to hide in until Automatons pass by (save the game while hiding).

Your father provides much information, including a spell and the name of the Island of the Nameless Masters.

Exit the dungeon the way you came in, and return the keys to Summa.

OBDEL

As you leave the Palace you will see a scroll at the entrance.

Visit Obdel, who wants your help, in the room south of Summa.

He offers a ring that will transport you into the Vizier's quarters.

In the Vizier's quarters, go west into the Harem, then to the Caliph's Bedroom and into a secret room to get a Journal and your family fortune.

(You must save after every successful foray.)

In the southwest corner of the palace, go to the small room with blue marks on the floor and activate the ring.

You emerge in one of the Vizier's rooms (you'll see an aide).

Slip out the west side (note the sleeping man), open the cabinet and read the scroll.

Go west, just to the door's edge.

If a guard is there, wait until he leaves, then follow him and get behind one of the columns in the hall to hide completely.

Save the game.

As he passes, go west and south — do not go into the room.

Click on the coffee table and push it, then go south to the Harem.

THE HAREM

Tell her your name is Catspaw, or whatever Obdel has told you.

She will give you a key and distract the guards.

Get behind the door, and watch out for the Jar: touch it, and you'll be captured.

Save the game.

When the lady gives you the signal, go north into the vestibule until you see the feet of the first guard going east.

Go north into the Caliph's Bedroom.

Go east and use the key on the secret door.

Open the chest and take the Journal.

Put the key under the mattress and go to the door.

Wait until the first guard comes up, turns and leaves.

Follow him and hide behind a column.

When he passes, go east and back to the Vizier's room where you first arrived.

Activate the ring in the southeast corner.

When you go back to talk to Obdel, he is gone.

The other man in the room tells you he went to his private chamber.

Go there, but you won't find him.

Now leave the castle and go to the city entrance.

Hide behind a tree and listen to the conversation.

When the Barbarian leaves, threaten him and get information about Al'katraz Island.

Take your boat and go to the Isle of Hajar.

THE ISLE OF HAJAR

Go east to the row of columns and follow the columns south to a Cyclops.

Slay him, then follow the path, killing any other Cyclops.

Stop before the path opens into an area to the north, where there are many lightning bolts.

Go into the field and keep healing yourself: do so each time you are hit.

Head for the chest, which disappears when you touch it, then reappears elsewhere.

After you touch it three times, the lightning bolts stop.

Take the treasure from the chest and go to the Isle of Al'Katraz.

THE ISLE OF AL'KATRAZ

You arrive at the north end of the island, where the tribes are feuding.

Go to the southwest and ask the leader ask why they are feuding, then tell them your story.

Tell the leader that you will speak to the other tribe's leader (always talk about the feud until it is settled).

After the two leaders agree on peace, they tell you that to reach the dungeons below, you must get a key from the two fires at the north part of the island.

Go to the two shrines in the south part of each side and meditate, and you will receive two words: Hama and Bazan.

Go to the southern well and speak these words into the blackness, and the well will open.

Enter the dungeons.

THE DUNGEONS

Immediately head west and follow the corridor around and to the south to a man in a large room.

Slay him and proceed west.

Follow the hall to a room with three men and slay them.

Go north until you hear laughing guards.

Enter the room and slay them, then go into the room to the northwest.

Kill all the guards in this room and proceed through the spiked, sealed west door into the catacombs.

THE CATACOMBS

Shake the door, and the spikes fall out.

Either slay all the monsters or leave the island.

Your job is done when you release your brother and kill the guards.

If you decide to proceed further, do not open the last cell in the southwest, which houses an undefeatable Ettin (but read the proper Scroll backwards, and the Ettin will disappear).

At this point your brother will follow you.

Return to the ship, take your brother down to the hold and leave him there.

Now go to the Isle of Aballat.

ISLE OF ABALLAT

Your goal here is to get your brother's voice back.

When you arrive, note the building with six doors to the north.

Ignore it for now and go around the building, releasing stoppers from the bottles that are hidden in the bushes.

One of the stoppers will be your brother's.

Now you can explore the building and kill anyone who prevents you from releasing the contents of any bottle.

Return to the boat and talk with Tarik, who will summon the Genie and break the curse by repeating the words backwards.

Now head for Al Naqqil.

AL NAQQIL: ISLAND OF THE NAMELESS ONES

Bring as many potions and spells as you can purchase; you will acquire some on the island.

Just north of where you begin are two barriers of flames and arrows.

Pull the west switch, then the east one.

Push the west switch again, then the east one, and the flames and arrows will stop.

Go north, then west and kill all the Nas Nas.

After each encounter, break something or cut the banner, so you will not have to bother with this room again.

Be sure and get the necklace, which is Master Necklace #1.

Go through the secret wall in the southeast corner and get the treasure.

Enter the rooms east of the hall and slay the Cyclops and the Wizard.

Break every container and open all cabinets, but do not read any books with runes on them, for they will cause you damage.

Exit this room and go north until you reach a large red and gold Jar.

Break the Jar, then enter the rooms to the east.

27

THE CYCLOPS

There are two rooms, each containing a Cyclops that must be killed.

Get the treasure from the large Jars in these rooms, then open both cabinets and read the scrolls.

Exit via the northeast corner and follow the hall north to a hall going east.

When you enter the hall, a Wizard will pop out of a secret wall to your north.

Slay him and get the necklace, which is Master Necklace #2.

Go west until you find a door to the north and a pair of Wizards you must kill (again, do not open books with runes on them).

Open the drawer to the north and read the scrolls, breaking all you find.

Go west out of this room until it turns to the south.

Walk close to the western side of the wall.

Watch closely for a fluctuation in the wall south of you, which indicates a secret doorway.

Go west until you are in a north-south hall.

Go north, slay the Wizard in the hall, then go around west into a room.

In this room you must slay another Wizard, after which you will obtain Master Necklace #3.

Read all the books in this room, then go south out of this room through a secret wall passage.

Go east through another secret wall.

Go south in the next hall and through a secret passage to the west.

Go north and take the treasure from the chest, then go north to an energy field that will transport you to a round island in the sky.

ISLAND IN THE SKY

Go northeast on the pathway.

Break the globe in the center of the island and kill the Cyclops that shows up.

Go to the northeast and break another globe.

Kill the Ogrima, then walk back to the southeast.

The path will now continue southeast to a new circle.

Break the globe and slay the man who appears.

Go southwest to a new island, then southwest to a path leading southeast and follow it to another island.

Break the globe and slay the mummy, which leaves a man for whom you will return later.

Now go northeast again to the place where you killed the man, then go southeast to another island.

THE GREAT GHOUL

Break the globe and slay the Great Ghoul.

Follow the path northeast to another island, where you will find a Moonstone that will completely cure you.

Leave via the northwest path to a dead end, then return, take a northeast path to a dead end and return.

Now take the path southeast to another island.

Break the globe and slay the Ettin.

Take the northwest path back to the Moonstone.

Heal yourself and take the northeast passage to a dead end.

On your way back from the dead end, a new path appears to the northeast appears.

Go up this path to another island.

Break the globe, and the Captain will arrive at your ship.

Go northeast and, and you will be transported to the hold of the ship.

Talk to the Captain, who swears that he will serve you forever.

THE NAMELESS MASTERS

(In the endgame, you will go back and slay the rest of the Nameless Masters, returning by going back to the ship's hold and through the bulkhead.)

You arrive on another island, from which you go northwest to new island.

Break the globe and slay the monster, then leave via the northwest to another island.

Break the globe to summon your duplicate, then slay him.

Save the game at once, as a Nameless Master will appear.

Use a Sun Dazzle Spell in the battle with the Nameless Master.

Exit via the southwest path, which is not complete: just walk back and forth on it until it extends no further, then go back to the Island and walk on the two new paths that appear.

The original pathway will now be extended to the southeast, so follow it to another Island.

Break the globe, and you will have to defeat a Great Ghoul.

After you do so, the Ghoul will turn into Princess Kara.

Talk to her, then leave her on the island and proceed down a southeast path to an empty island.

From the empty island, go southeast to another island and the last Nameless Master.

Slay him, again using a Lightning or Sun Dazzle.

After you finish off the last Nameless Master, the Genie will appear.

Take care of the people you left on the islands and get the Princess, and the quest concludes.

ORBS & STUFF

Object	See this Section for Location	Also See Section(s)
Berries	Zaratan & the Berries	Location only
Healing potions	Zaratan & the Berries, Deadman's Reef	Bandar Al-Sa'adat, Isle of Shabaz
Parchment	The Treaty	Location only
Small key	Deadman's Reef	Location only
Large key	Deadman's Reef	Location only
Green key	Deadman's Reef	Location only
Oil	Deadman's Reef	Location only
Ring of Protection +1	Bandar Al-Sa'adat	Location only
Treasure	Sorcerer Al'Mutan's Tower, Room of Circles, The Spikes, The Seals, Isle of Hajar, Al Naqqil, The Cyclops	Locations only
Singing Scimitar	The Singing Scimitar	Location only
Wisest Snake in World	The Efreet's Missions	Location only
Hottest Coal in World	The Efreet's Missions	Location only
Veil made by Indrind	The Efreet's Missions	Location only
Bottle of Emptiness (Vial)	Isle of Senat	Location only
Shahar I Zade	The Genie Gem	Location only
Genie Gem	The Genie Gem	Location only
Sky Gem	The Genie Gem	Location only
Key for Wine Cellar	Caliph's Palace	Location only
Bone key	Caliph's Palace	Location only
Scroll	Obdel	Location only
Master Necklace #1	Al Naqqil	Location only
Master Necklace #2	The Cyclops	Location only
Master Necklace #3	The Cyclops	Location only

31

ALONE IN THE DARK II

BY

FRED PHILLIP & CLANCY SCHAFFER

TYPE
Animated Adventure

SYSTEM
IBM & IBM CD-ROM (Required: 386/33+ MHZ, 2 MB RAM, VGA, mouse, 14 MB hard disk)

COMPANY
I-Motion/ Interplay

DESCRIBED AS A "VIRTUAL 3-D MYSTERY," THE SEQUEL TO ONE OF 1993'S MOST INVENTIVE ANIMATED ADVENTURES DEFIES YOU TO BREAK INTO A HAUNTED MANSION RATHER THAN ESCAPE FROM ONE. ONCE YOU DO GET INSIDE, THE HOUSE TURNS OUT TO BE MUCH BIGGER AND FILLED WITH AS MANY COMBAT SITUATIONS AS WITH LOGICAL PUZZLES FOR YOU TO UNRAVEL. IN THE ROLE OF EDWARD CARNBY, YOU STRIVE TO FREE A LITTLE GIRL KIDNAPPED BY ONE EYED JACK, THE NEFARIOUS CRIME LORD. BUT THE STORY GOES BACK TO THE 1800'S, AS YOU DISCOVER ANCIENT VOODOO RITUALS IN HAITI THAT ARE STILL ALIVE TODAY.

PROGRESS THROUGH THIS MYSTERY IS MAINLY LINEAR, BUT YOU SWITCH BETWEEN PLAYING CARNBY AND THE GIRL IN LATER PARTS OF THE GAME, WHICH ADDS VARIETY TO THE QUEST. THE 3-D GRAPHICS PORTRAY THE SURROUNDINGS AND CHARACTERS WITH A FASCINATING VIEW THAT PULLS YOU RIGHT INTO THE ACTION. BUT MANY ADVENTURERS WILL FIND TOO MUCH ACTION,

COMPARED WITH THE ORIGINAL GAME, WHICH FOCUSED MAINLY ON LOGICAL PUZZLES. IN SHORT, YOU WILL DIE FREQUENTLY AND MUST RESTORE COUNTLESS SAVED GAMES ON THE ROAD TO SUCCESS. A SLICK DESIGN AND GORGEOUS 3-D GRAPHICS ARE THIS SEQUEL'S STRONG POINTS. ALONE IN THE DARK II IS AN ENGAGING MYSTERY THAT WILL BE MOST APPRECIATED BY THOSE WHO ENJOY FREQUENT COMBAT AS MUCH AS THEY DO FIGURING OUT HOW TO OPERATE THE CANNON AND WHERE TO FIND A SANTA CLAUS COSTUME.

THE SOLUTION

GENERAL

Conserve your ammo and health.

Pick up everything you find, as only a few items in the game are not needed.

Read everything you can read: books, notes, parchments, and so on, in order to appreciate the story.

You may have to replay many combat sequences until you get it just right.

Precise positioning is necessary both in combat and using objects.

Save often. All food and flasks increase health.

OUTSIDE MANSION

HEDGE MAZE

Kick or butt the first pirate to death.

Get the gun, clip and flask.

Load gun and drink flask.

Go along path to the bench and shoot the next two pirates. (This may take some doing.)

When you've finally killed them, move the bench aside and enter the maze.

Map all areas of the maze, killing pirates and other foes as you go.

Among other items, make sure you get a paper bag (behind the pirate you kill) and a rope.

At the spot with three cards on ground, stand on the red diamond to open the hole.

Get hook lying on ground and enter the hole.

THE STATUE

Push the chest and get the metallic Jack of Diamonds.

Kill all intruders. Get pirate sword.

Use metallic card (Jack of Diamonds) on altar to open trap door.

Go up ladder and into the hedge maze.

Locate the area with the moving branches blocking your way and hack them off with the sword.

Continue on to the statue, kill the monster there, then go to the statue where the monster was and get the newspaper page.

Use hook on the rope, use grappling hook on statue, and climb down hole.

DEAD TED

Pick up the nickel and crank (at north side of plank).

Search the dead body and get page and pipe cleaner.

Put newspaper under locked door near body.

Use pipe cleaner on lock, remove paper, get key, unlock door.

SECRET PASSAGE

Enter, walk south and kill pirate (or stand to left of lever, blow up and pop paper bag you found in the maze behind the pirate.

Then use the lever to knock him through the hole behind him with a flying barrel that appears).

Use crank in hole in clock.

Pick up book.

Go north to the wall behind the boxes, which is now open.

Enter, take elevator up, kill pirate, get hook.

INSIDE MANSION

BASEMENT

Explore and get battledore (weapon). Kill anything that moves.

At the cards, turn all cards to Red Diamonds to open the locked door next to cards.

Kill the pirate who emerges and enter storeroom.

Get the flask, whiskey bottle and two books.

Put nickel in slot machine to get two pipe organ tokens.

Exit room.

Near the next door is a monster and sack.

Kill the monster, pick up sack, use sack and wear Santa Claus outfit.

Exit basement and go upstairs.

FIRST FLOOR

At the statue, get the crown, avoiding trident the statue will throw at you when you step on a trigger block on the floor.

Enter kitchen.

Near oven, get poison.

Get fried eggs from counter and eat them.

Get the frying pan and exit kitchen.

Stand outside door and kill Chef with frying pan as he emerges.

At the sink, get wine.

Use poison in wine.

Exit kitchen.

PIPE ORGAN

Use poisoned wine on closed doors in statue room. This will open the door and wipe out the two pirates who emerge from the room. Enter.

Put both tokens in pipe organ to open other door in room.

Pick up doubloon on floor.

Enter opened room.

Get and wear armored vest.

Exit and go to stairs up. Up.

UPSTAIRS

Kill pirate.

Go to Billiards room.

Kill pirate, get derringer, sword-stick, book and piece of parchment.

Go to bedroom.

Slice off hands in corner of room and get second piece of parchment regarding the Amulet.

Put crown on Queen's bust.

Enter back room and pick up Amulet.

You will be teleported to the attic.

THE ATTIC

Exit room.

Wipe out Acrobat and Henchman.

Get grenade and flask.

Pick up Gold Key.

Go around corner to chest for a Thompson machine-gun and clip.

Enter open room and put doubloon in Jack in the Box to get Pom Pom.

Open closed door; ignore Jester.

Stand in front of lattice door and throw Pom Pom into garden.

Move aside to let Jester enter garden, and he will be wiped out by the snakes in the garden.

Enter garden, drop grenade down chimney in corner and climb down.

BACK DOWNSTAIRS

Kill three pirates (the grenade blew away the two others). This is difficult, so keep trying.

Try to get in between two of them and let them shoot at each other.

When they're finally dead, get the red billiard ball off the Christmas tree.

BACK UPSTAIRS

Proceed to the billiard room and put red billiard ball in device with all the pegs and holes.

This will slide the bookcase on your left aside, revealing a door.

Unlock door with Gold Key and open door to enter.

You will now be in a cell.

CAPTURED

One Eyed Jack, in a series of still shots, will tell you about the Flying Dutchman and Hell's Kitchen. Grace is also in the room.

After One Eyed Jack and Grace leave, use hook on green door to exit cell.

You will be in the Captain's bedroom.

Exiting room will take you back to the billiard room.

STORY TIME

Go downstairs and head for the kitchen. Elisabeth Jarret, a witch, will appear. In a series of still shots, she will tell you about Haiti, slaves and Cotten. She will tell you that she made the crew of the Flying Dutchman immortal and that every 100 years a young girl would be selected to grow old as part of the ritual. Jarret will fly away, and you find yourself shackled in the hold of a ship.

At this point you take on the persona of Grace, carrying a teddy bear.

GRACE

ON SHIP

Move the board that blocks the opening to your left.

Enter the room with the parrot.

Get the sandwich and eat it.

Get pepperpot and bag of seeds.

Give seeds to parrot for clue regarding the Captain's staff.

Check out the map on the wall.

Exit to hall. Go back up into room until the pirate passes.

Go out, then right to the ladder and up.

Go up the next ladder to deck.

DECK

Moving clockwise, sneak behind the boxes and barrels until you are behind the barrel next to the open hatch in deck.

Turn around. Move back.

Get tinder box.

Move forward, turn and jump down hatch. (This is a difficult sequence and may take several tries.)

CAPTAIN'S CABIN

Open the chest to get the small cannon.

Get crystal vase from the cabinet.

Check closet and get Captain's staff.

Note statue of Captain Nichols.

Drop the small cannon near door.

Use pepperpot on cannon.

Throw vase.

Use tinder box on cannon to blow away pirate who enters the room.

Back in the basement in Alone in the Dark 2

DUMBWAITER

Exit cabin and pick up the bell.

Go through open door and grab the chicken foot.

Use bell to call dumbwaiter up.

Enter dumbwaiter to descend.

RETURN TO MANSION

KITCHEN

Pick up key on floor and unlock cabinet on the wall.

Get ice box and pot of molasses.

To wipe out pirate chasing you, run out of kitchen, turn around and drop ice at doorway.

Go upstairs and drop molasses on north edge of carpet to stick next pirate in place.

UPSTAIRS AGAIN

Go to billiards room and get token.

Go to Captain's cabin.

Use staff on desk. (This changes staff to the Loa Staff.)

Get a book and a key to the irons.

Read book.

Go to bedroom and use the staff on symbol on floor in back room.

You will find Grace back downstairs.

DOWNSTAIRS

Enter the kitchen and quickly exit.

The pirate will follow you, slip on the ice you dumped near the door and break his neck.

Enter kitchen, ring bell to summon dumbwaiter, and ride up.

You will find yourself in the ship's hold.

SHIP'S HOLD

You are now Carnby again.

Hold down the right arrow key until Carnby picks up the key.

As Carnby, use the key to unlock the shackles.

Fight and kill the pirate. Get his sword.

CARNBY

LOWER DECK

Equip sword, exit through door and slay the next pirate.

Exit next door, kill the next pirate and get the short fuse.

There are doors to the north, northeast and east, and a locked door to the southeast with ladders going up. Each room is guarded by pirates.

FOUR ROOMS

The room to the north contains a flask and ammo. The one to the northeast has a flask, pistol, vest and ammo.

Move barrel to get another vest and a bottle.

Throw bottle to break it and get a parchment.

The east room contains a poker, pliers and a key in the corner.

Unlock the southeast room with key.

Get keg of powder and opuscule (book).

You are in the powder room. For some fun, use a firearm in here (save first).

Exit and climb up ladder to the upper deck.

UPPER DECK

CANNON

Note the locked doors and bunk room with sleeping pirates.

Enter the room with the cannon and slay the pirate.

Use pliers on the chain.

Face cannon, looking north in the center of cannon, and press space bar to move cannon into position.

Cross the hall to the bunk room and place keg on floor near the circle.

Return to the cannon and use short fuse on cannon.

Use poker on fuse to blow up keg in bunk room.

This will not only blow up the bunk room, but the pirates as well.

Go to the bunk room and look around for a pouch of gold coins and a flask.

Go to the locked doors and use coins.

Two chefs will come out of kitchen.

Kill them.

Enter kitchen and pick up flask.

LOCKED DOOR

In the kitchen, the door to the freezer is now open.

Enter and slay the chef.

Get a metallic Jack of Diamonds.

Exit kitchen and go to the locked door across the hall.

Use Jack of Diamonds to unlock the door.

This will cut away to a shot of Jarret suspended on a ceiling.

You will now be transformed back to Grace.

GRACE AGAIN

WITCH HUNTING

You will find yourself, as Grace, back in the Captain's bedroom.

You will be carrying the chicken foot and Loa Staff.

Walk to the statue and use Loa Staff to open door next to statue.

Enter next room.

You will be in the quarters of Jarret the Witch, who is about to zap you.

Instead, go to cabinet with skull on top and use the chicken foot. This will zap Jarret out of existence.

You will see Grace entering a lifeboat at the side of the ship. Carnby will fall off the ceiling in the Captain's bedroom. Once again, you are Carnby.

BACK AS CARNBY

MAIN DECK

Quickly exit the room to escape the Giant Pirate who is attacking you.

Take the ladder up to the main deck.

You will have a major fight on your hands. Kill all the pirates and get the hook. If you watched closely, you would have seen one pirate grab a sword from the deck and flee, and another climb up the mast.

CAPTAIN NICHOLS' SWORD

Climb up the main mast and kill the pirate on top.

Use the hook on the rope to swing down to the lower mast.

The pirate who grabbed the sword from the deck will now attack you. Kill him.

Jump down from the mast to the deck and pick up Captain Nichols' sword.

END GAME

Run to Grace, who is now shackled to the main mast.

Cut the chains with the pliers.

Run to cannons on deck and touch them to disarm.

Use Captain Nichols' sword to kill One Eyed Jack.

COMBAT TIPS

Stand between the cannons facing Jack.

Lunge at Jack, then step back.

Lunge, step back.

Continue to repeat until Jack is dead (or so it would seem).

ORBS & STUFF

Object	See this Section for Location	Also See Section(s)
Clip	Hedge Maze, The Attic	Locations only
Flask	Hedge Maze, Basement, Attic, Four Rooms	Locations only
Gun	Hedge Maze	Location only
Hook	Hedge Maze, Secret Passage, Main Deck	The Statue, Captured, Captain Nichol's Sword
Rope	Hedge Maze	Hedge Maze, The Statue, Captain Nichol's Sword
Jack of Diamonds	The Statue, Locked Door	Locations only
Newspaper page	The Statue	Dead Ted
Nickel	Dead Ted	Basement
Crank	Dead Ted	Secret Passage
Page	Dead Ted	Location only
Pirate Sword	The Statue	The Statue, Ship's Hold, Lower Deck
Pipe Cleaner	Dead Ted	Location only
Paper Bag	Hedge Maze	Secret Passage
Book(s)	Secret Passage, Basement, Upstairs, Upstairs Again, Four Rooms	Locations only
Flying Barrel	Secret Passage	Location only
Battledore	Basement	Location only
Bottle(s)	Basement, Four Rooms	Four Rooms
Tokens	Basement, Upstairs Again	Pipe Organ
Sack	Basement	Location only
Santa Claus outfit	Basement	Location only
Crown	First Floor	Location only
Poison	First Floor	First floor, Pipe Organ
Fried eggs	First Floor	Location only
Frying pan	First Floor	Location only
Wine	First Floor	Pipe Organ
Doubloon	Pipe Organ	The Attic
Armored vest	Pipe Organ, Four Rooms	Locations only
Derringer	Upstairs	Location only
Parchment(s)	Upstairs, Four Rooms	Location only

44

Amulet	Upstairs	Location only
Grenade	The Attic	The Attic, Back Downstairs
Gold Key	The Attic	Back Upstairs
Machine-gun	The Attic	Location only
Pom Pom	The Attic	Location only
Billiard ball	Back Downstairs	Back Upstairs
Parrot	On Ship	Location only
Captain's staff (Loa)	Captain's Cabin	On Ship, Upstairs Again, Witch Hunting
Tinder Box	Deck	Captain's Cabin
Cannon	Captain's Cabin, Cannon	Locations only
Pepperpot	On Ship	Captain's Cabin
Map	On Ship	Location only
Vase	Captain's Cabin	Location only
Bell	Dumbwaiter	Dumbwaiter, Witch Hunting
Chicken foot	Dumbwaiter	Witch Hunting
Ice Box & ice	Kitchen	Location only
Molasses	Kitchen	Location only
Fuse	Lower Deck	Cannon
Powder keg	Four Rooms	Cannon
Poker	Four Rooms	Cannon
Pliers	Four Rooms	Cannon, End Game
Cannon	Cannon	Location only

THE CALL OF CTHULHU: SHADOW OF THE COMET

BY
PAUL SHAFFER

TYPE
Animated Adventure

SYSTEM
IBM CD (Required: 386/16+, 2 MB RAM, 512K EMS, 256-color VGA, hard disk, CD-ROM drive 150 K /sec. minimum, MSCDEX 2.2+, Sound Blaster or compatible, mouse)

COMPANY
I-Motion/ Interplay

H. P. LOVECRAFT WOULD HAVE APPRECIATED THE STRANGE INTERFACE AND GRAPHICS OF *SHADOW OF THE COMET*, WHICH WAS INSPIRED BY THE CTHULHU MYTHOS THAT FORMED THE CORNERSTONE OF HIS MOST UNSETTLING HORROR STORIES. IT TAKES PLACE IN 1910, THE SAME ERA AS LOVECRAFT'S TALES. ACCORDINGLY, THE ILLUSTRATIONS LOOK LIKE ANIMATED EMBROIDERY. AFTER ALL THE SLICK DIGITIZED ART AND VISUAL EFFECTS THAT TYPIFY ADVENTURE GAME GRAPHICS, THIS IS A RELIEF TO THE EYE. YOU PLAY THE PART OF AN ASTRONOMER WHO VISITS THE NEW ENGLAND TOWN OF ILLSMOUTH TO INVESTIGATE A UNIQUE STELLAR PHENOMENON DISCOVERED 76 YEARS AGO BY LORD BOLESKINE, WHO MYSTERIOUSLY WENT MAD AT THE APPEARANCE OF HALEY'S COMET. TO PROVE HIS DISCOVERY, YOU BRING ALONG ONE OF THE EARLY CAMERAS A FEW DAYS BEFORE THE COMET'S NEXT APPEARANCE. THE STORY UNFOLDS

IN THREE ONE-DAY ACTS IN WHICH YOU STUMBLE ACROSS THE SOURCE OF BOLESKIN'S MADNESS — A SINISTER CULT WORSHIPPING CTHULHU, AN UNHUMAN HORROR THAT ONCE RULED EARTH AND PLANS TO RETURN. MOVEMENT IS IN FOUR DIRECTIONS ONLY, WHICH CAN BE AWKWARD, BUT THE AUTO-MAPPING AND AUTO-NOTEPAD ARE HANDY. THIS GAME HAS ITS OWN DEFINITION OF "POINT AND CLICK" THAT IS UNFAMILIAR. WHEN YOU CLICK ON A LOOK ICON TO EXAMINE AN OBJECT, ITS DESCRIPTION APPEARS IN YOUR NOTEBOOK INSTEAD OF IN AN IMMEDIATE ONSCREEN DISPLAY. THE GAME INCLUDES A SEPARATE PROGRAM IN WHICH YOU TAKE A SELF-GUIDED TOUR OF A "LOVECRAFT MUSEUM" FULL OF WEIRD EXHIBITS AND, AS LOVECRAFT LOVED TO CALL THEM, "ELDRITCH HORRORS."

THE SOLUTION

DAY ONE

GETTING STARTED

At the docks, walk to Arlington and Cobble.

In front of the lodge, use responses 1, 1.

In room, get Boleskine's diary and telegram, then read both.

Look in chest and drawer.

Go to the store and talk to clerk: answer 1 (getting photo plates).

Go to hall in town records and examine writing on small statue.

In records room, talk to Juggs (twice): respond with 1, 2.

Walk to register at right of room and examine it (getting names).

Talk to Juggs again: 2, 1.

Return to hall (Juggs leaves).

Reenter records and look in all four cabinets at rear of room (getting magnifying glass).

CURTIS HAMBLETON

Go to fishery by the docks.

Get rope ladder from garbage.

Enter fishery.

Talk to Hambleton: 1.

GYPSIES

Go to the park.

Talk to officer (twice)

JUGG'S

Go to Jugg's home and go to room with the rifle.

Examine rifle.

Use magnifying glass with rifle.

Go to study and talk to Jugg: 3.

PREPARING FOR THE SHOOT

Go into woods and get three branches and a creeper (see map).

Return to lodge room.

Open chest and get drawing and map.

Open drawer and get cotton and surgical spirit.

Use spirit on cotton.

Go to desk and use drawing.

Use cotton on drawing.

Get rubbed drawing.

While still at the table, use the map.

Move hand (with the cursor keys) to the Searcher constellation and mark it.

FINDING A GUIDE

Go to the pharmacy entrance and talk to the clerk.

Go to the tavern entrance and talk to Cobble.

Enter tavern and go to the bar.

Talk to the bartender twice (Tyler enters and you sit).

Use responses: 2, 2.

The window breaks and everyone goes outside.

Pick up bat.

Use bat with Hambleton boys (go to drugstore).

THE CALVARY

Return to room.

Open chest and get camera, tripod, lantern and lens.

Go to town hall and talk to Matthews (go to bridge).

Cross bridge.

At the cross, use set of photo plates.

Make tripod by using three branches and creeper.

Use camera.

Use all three photo plates.

Go east and look at bushes (noting passage).

Enter passage and immediately move right to hide behind tree (getting parchment).

When discovered, run back across the bridge.

DAY TWO

DEVELOPING THE PRINTS

Get prescription from the table and read it.

Read parchment.

Go to pharmacy and give prescription to doctor.

Go to supply room and take all chemicals (four from the counter and four from top of the ladder).

Go west into the darkroom.

Walk to the light at rear of the room (this turns off the light).

Go to the developing trays and use exposed plates.

Use Metol, Hydroquinone, Sodium Thiosulphate and Potash Metabisulfite (viewing developed prints).

INTERPRETING THE PARCHMENT

Go to Jugg's place and follow Hambleton into the store.

Get the key he leaves on the counter.

Return to Jugg's and use key on front door.

In the first room, get the statue of a baby.

In the second room, examine the small cabinet and get the statue of a young man.

In the third room, examine the small butterfly display and get the statue of an old man.

Enter study, get "Youth" book from bookcase and replace it with statue of baby.

Get "Old Man and the Sea" from shelf and replace it with statue of old man.

Get "Invisible Man" from shelf and replace it with statue of young man.

(If you picked up any other titles, replace them.)

This will open the bookcase.

THE SECRET LIBRARY

Enter the secret library and talk to Juggs.

Use parchment on Juggs.

Get message from desk.

Get Necronomicon.

Return to study and examine left side of carpet (getting small key).

Return to the secret library and use small key on Necronomicon.

Read Necronomicon.

Use Necronomicon again to replace it.

Examine books on back shelves.

RECOVERING THE DIARY

Return directly home and read the message in your lodge room.

Go to the post office, enter and talk to Ms. Gilcrest: 1.

Go out the back door and talk to Underhouse.

Outside the post office, talk to Ms. Pickott twice: 1.

Go to the store and talk to the clerk: 3 (getting brooch, locket and plates).

Return to Pickott and use brooch on her, then the locket (getting Bible).

Examine Bible: 3 (noting page number 345).

Go to the Mayor's office.

Talk to Mr. Swig: 2, 3, 1.

Enter office.

Examine painting (you discover the safe).

Examine safe.

Enter 345 (use cursor keys to switch dials).

Get diary and cigar case.

Examine cigar case (getting deposit note).

Examine deposit note.

Examine diary (returning it to safe when done).

Quaint New England town where the horror coalesces.

....

REACHING THE LIGHTHOUSE

Go to the post office.

Give deposit note to Ms. Gilcrest (getting parcel).

Exit post office and open parcel (getting frock).

Go to well, walk behind it and change into frock.

Go east to lighthouse: 1.

Open gate.

At lighthouse door, look.

Go to right side of lighthouse and change back into old clothes.

Use rope ladder by windows.

At top of lighthouse, examine sun dial (opening mechanism).

Get wings.

Examine other opening and get candle.

Use candle.

Use magnifying glass on candle.

Move glass (with cursor keys) over candle to light it.

Use candle on wings, then use wings.

GYPSY CAMP

Walk to crystal ball.

Talk to woman (you see vision).

GETTING INTO CEMETERY

Talk to Bishop in front of pharmacy: 1, 1.

Talk to him again (getting cemetery key).

Go to cemetery (using key to unlock gates).

Explore cemetery (getting rope and bar).

Enter crypt.

Use bar on gate.

Use rope on opening.

Climb down rope.

THE LABYRINTH

Go east and get skull.

West. West (avoid bat).

West (avoid spikes by staying to sides of room).

Go north and get skull.

Return to rope and go north.

Use both skulls on pedestals.

Go north (avoid pit).

Go west and south (avoid spiders and walk over hidden floor panel).

North. West.

Illuminate all four panels by walking over them in this order: southeast, northeast, northwest, southwest.

THE FOUR STATUES

Walk off the panels.

North. East.

Get the first and second statues.

Put the first statue in the niche where you got the second one, and vice versa (which a opens secret door).

North. West (activates hidden panel).

Go: east, east, east, south, south (avoid pit).

South (avoid spiders).

South (avoid bat).

East (activate floor panel).

Return to the last hidden pit room.

Go east, south, east, south and south.

Walk around hole until hidden door appears, then go west.

Activate floor panel.

Go east, north, north, north.

Save the game.

Step on the following squares to make them all light up: southeast, east, northeast, north, northwest, west, southwest, south.

Exit the squares.

Go north, west, north.

Read each plaque (left to right).

Walk around table three times, then go east.

Save game and go north.

Take all four statues.

Run away!

Run back to labyrinth entrance (all traps are no longer active, but don't use any stairs or you'll be stuck).

Climb rope (taken to Webster's house).

THE FAMILY SIGN

Examine painting on the left wall.

Examine drawing.

Talk to Ms. Webster.

THE FAMILY SANCTIONS

Go to Tyler Inn.

When Tyler approaches, use first statue.

Say IAE YOG THU SOT.

Walk onto revealed symbol and use first statue again (kills Tyler).

Go to Arlington's barn.

Use second statue.

Say RLA GNA HAS TEP.

Climb rope to symbol.

Use second statue again (killing Arlington).

Go to Coldstone's (walking to west side of house before using statue).

Use third statue.

Say NGH HLU KHU WIG.

Walk to symbol and use statue again (killing Coldstone).

THE HAMBLETON SANCTION

Go to store entrance.

Get rotten fish from garbage.

Walk to middle of screen and use fish (getting cat).

Go to Hambleton house by way of Bishop's place.

Use cat on dog.

Run east, north, west, west, south, south.

Enter abandoned Hambleton ruin.

Get compass card from left drawer.

Get lantern.

Use compass card on ship's wheel.

Go up and use lantern on fireplace.

Go up and examine desk along south wall twice.

Get handle and use on telescope.

Examine southernmost lever (using it and getting ball).

Use ball on wall painting.

Examine books and read "Magic Rites."

Go up and use fourth statue.

Say THO NYA CHT TUR.

Get caught and, when about to be stabbed, use statue again.

Run out of building before it catches fire.

DAY THREE

FINDING AN ALIBI

Go to Cobble and use response 1.

Read message.

At lodge entrance, talk to Pickott: 1.

Got straight to Underhouse in post office.

When policeman enters: 1, 1 (he gives you feather).

BOW AND ARROW

Go to fishery.

Talk to Bishop.

Take stick.

Use stick on door.

Use brooch, getting pin.

Use pin on padlock.

Enter and examine Curtis.

Examine fireplace.

Get bow.

Examine table (noticing gash).

Examine floor panels in lower left of room (getting arrow).

Go to spot in forest where you got creeper.

Put feather on stump (taken to Natawanga).

NATAWANGA'S QUIZ

1. Mic-Macs
2. Yog Suthoth
3. 1834
4. Star
5. Dagon

NIRAKAMUS' SANCTION

Before you are returned, Natawanga gives you a pot of paint and ring.

Go to well and examine it (you enter).

Go east and throw pot of paint into water.

Go east and get empty can and can of acid.

Go east and get two flints.

Use empty can on pool of naphtha.

Go south and use can of naphtha.

Use flints.

Use bow (ghost sequence).

Get turquoise, aquamarine and butterfly.

Refill empty can with naphtha on your way out.

Use turquoise on Natawanga's ring.

GETTING A BOAT

Go to the docks.

Save the game.

Talk to Bishop: 2, 3, 3, 2.

Walk to boat.

BINDING DRAGON

On the island, get emerald and ruby.

Examine stone carving (the columns are up and down, rows are side to side.)

Move third column down twice.

Move fourth row to left once.

Move second column down once.

Move third row left twice.

Enter and use ruby on statue.

Stand on star where the fifth point of the ray should fall.

Use aquamarine.

Outside, the ghost of Boleskine will give you his ring.

Get back in boat.

TEMPLE OF CTHULHU

Enter cavern.

Use lantern and enter (when oil runs out, use can of naphtha).

Go west, then north (avoid creatures).

Use can of acid on center of room, getting diamond.

Use emerald on Boleskine's ring.

Use Boleskine's and Natawanga's rings.

Go south, then east.

Go east and look for hidden opening in northeast part of room.

STONE CIRCLE: ENDGAME

Use tripod.

Use set of photo plates (unwraps).

Use camera.

Use butterfly (twice).

Use magnifying glass.

Use lantern.

Save the game.

Use plates.

Get fragment of comet.

Use aquamarine on blue spot.

Use diamond on green spot.

Use comet fragment on white spot.

Use flints on red spot.

ORBS & STUFF

Object	See this Section for Location	Also See Section(s)
Boleskine's diary	Getting Started	Location only
Telegram	Getting Started	Location only
Photo plates	Getting Started	The Calvary, Developing the Prints, Recovering the Diary, Stone Circle
Rope ladder	Curtis Hambleton	Reaching the Lighthouse
Three branches	Preparing for the Shoot	The Calvary
Creeper	Preparing for the Shoot	The Calvary
Map	Preparing for the Shoot	Location only
Drawing	Preparing for the Shoot	The Family Sign
Surgical spirit	Preparing for the Shoot	Location only
Cotton	Preparing for the Shoot	Location only
Bat	Finding a Guide	Location only
Camera	The Calvary	Stone Circle
Tripod	The Calvary	Stone Circle
Lantern	The Calvary	The Hambleton Sanction, Temple of Cthulhu, Stone Circle
Lens	The Calvary	Location only
Parchment	The Calvary	Developing the Prints, Interpreting the Parchment, The Secret Library
Prescription	Developing the Prints	Location only
Chemicals	Developing the Prints	Location only
Key to Jugg's place	Interpreting the Parchment	Location only
Four statues	Interpreting the Parchment	Location only
Necronomican	The Secret Library	Location only
Brooch	Recovering the Diary	Bow and Arrow
Locket	Recovering the Diary	Location only
Photo plates	Recovering the Diary	Stone Circle
Deposit note	Recovering the Diary	Reaching the Lighthouse
Frock	Reaching the Lighthouse	Location only
Wings	Reaching the Lighthouse	Location only
Cemetery key	Getting into Cemetery	Location only
Rope	Getting into Cemetery	The Four Statues
Bar	Getting into Cemetery	Location only

Four More Statues	The Four Statues	The Family Sanctions, The Hambleton Sanction
Compass card	The Hambleton Sanction	Location only
Telescope	The Hambleton Sanction	Location only
Ball	The Hambleton Sanction	Location only
Feather	Finding an Alibi	Bow and Arrow
Bow	Bow and Arrow	Nirakamus' Sanction
Aquamarine	Nirakamus' Sanction	Binding Dragon
Turqouise	Nirakamus' Sanction	Location only
Butterfly	Nirakamus' Sanction	Stone Circle
Naphtha	Nirakamus' Sanction	Temple of Cthulhu
Boleskine's ring	Binding Dragon	Temple of Cthulhu
Diamond	Temple of Cthulhu	Stone Circle
Comet fragment	Stone Circle	Location only
Natawanga's Ring	Nirakamus' Sanction	Temple of Cthulhu

Shadow of the Comet

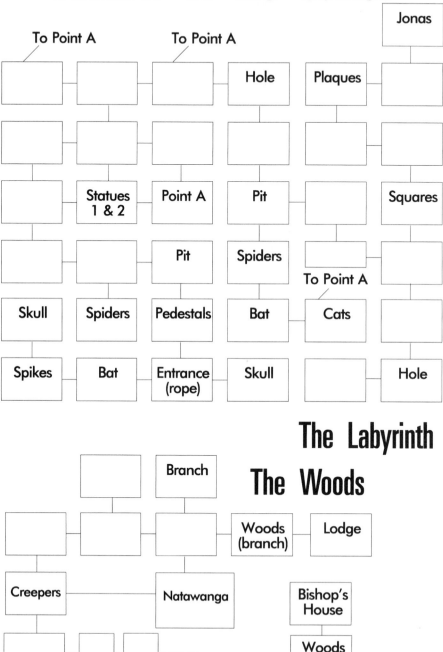

To Point A

To Point A

| | | | Hole | Plaques | Jonas |

| | | | | | |

| | Statues 1 & 2 | Point A | Pit | | Squares |

| | | Pit | Spiders | | |

| Skull | Spiders | Pedestals | Bat | Cats | |

| Spikes | Bat | Entrance (rope) | Skull | | Hole |

To Point A

The Labyrinth

The Woods

Branch

Woods (branch) — Lodge

Creepers — Natawanga

Bishop's House

Woods (branch)

THE ELDER SCROLLS: ARENA

BY
CLANCY SHAFFER
& FRED PHILIPP

TYPE
Fantasy Role-playing

SYSTEM
IBM (Required: 386/25+, DOS 5.0+, 4 MB RAM (2 MB EMS), 30 MB hard disk, 100% Microsoft-compatible mouse, VGA. Supports: Aria, Ensonique, Roland MT-32 & LAPC, Sound Blaster, Ultrasound. Recommended: 386/33+ and sound card)

COMPANY
Bethesda Toolworks

HE BIGGEST, THE BOLDEST, THE BEST — SINCE BETRAYAL AT KRONDOR, NO ROLE-PLAYING GAME HAS OFFERED SO MANY PLACES TO VISIT, SO MANY THINGS TO DO, SO MANY QUESTS TO COMPLETE, AND SUCH OUTSTANDING GRAPHICS AND SPECIAL EFFECTS. THE CHALLENGE IS TO COLLECT ALL EIGHT PIECES OF THE STAFF OF CHAOS AND FREE THE EMPEROR OF TAMRIEL FROM IMPRISONMENT IN ANOTHER DIMENSION. EACH OF THESE EIGHT MINI-QUESTS IS A MAJOR UNDERTAKING THAT IS AS INVOLVED AND TIME-CONSUMING AS SOME ENTIRE GAMES. AND IN ADDITION TO THE EIGHT MAIN MINI-QUESTS, THERE ARE NUMEROUS OTHER QUESTS YOU MAY PURSUE. THE PRESENTATION MIMICS THE 3-D STYLE OF ULTIMA UNDERWORLD, AND THE INTERFACE, WITH ITS "SMART CURSOR" THAT CHANGES SHAPE TO SUGGEST WHAT YOU CAN DO WITH OBJECTS, IS QUICKLY

MASTERED.

IN ADDITION TO DISCOVERING SPELLS, YOU CAN DESIGN THEM YOURSELF WITH THE SPELLMAKER BY ALLOTTING SPELL POINTS AND EFFECTS TO THE SPELL NAMES YOU COIN. SUCH A HIGH DEGREE OF PERSONALIZATION, BLENDED WITH ANIMATED EFFECTS AND BACKGROUND ART SO VIVID YOU ALMOST FEEL YOU ARE REALLY THERE, TRANSPORTS ARENA BEYOND THE REALM OF MERE ROLE-PLAYING AND INTO THE COMPUTER GAME HALL OF FAME. A BEST QUEST OF THE MONTH IN THE ROLE-PLAYING CATEGORY, ARENA IS A "MUST QUEST" FOR ALL RPG FANS.

THE SOLUTION

There are hundreds of side-quests in this game, but the main goal is to retrieve the eight parts of the Staff of Chaos in order to restore the rightful Emperor, a challenge that takes place in 16 mini-quests. For each piece of the Staff, you must first retrieve an object that enables a character to inscribe the location of the piece on your map, then obtain the piece itself from that location.

YOUR CHARACTER

The Spellsword, who wears chain armor and has the power of both a Warrior and Mage, is recommended. Save at least every two minutes in the first dungeon. In later dungeons, save at least every five to ten minutes.

Don't be greedy, or you will find yourself overburdened. Also, keep a couple of spots always available in your inventory. Do not buy over 99 Potions, but do buy all of the spells.

GOLD & GEAR

In the early parts of the game, it is very important to earn as much gold as possible to get enough armor, weapons, spells and magical items to survive in a dungeon. In at least the first town, spend a few game sessions going on mini-quests. They usually involve the delivery or retrieval of an object or person within the town, but dungeons in the wilderness pay the best. If you're lucky, you may just earn of one of the sixteen magical artifacts in the game during your sessions going on town quests. After a dungeon or two, you should have enough money to buy whatever you need.

In dungeons, always click on the bodies of dead monsters to find gold. You will gather much more gold in your dungeon jaunts if you exhaustively search the dungeon rather than just head for the door to the next level or the item or Staff piece you need.

It is very important to save the game before you leave any dungeons or go to a different dungeon level. *Arena* sometimes locks up or runs out of memory when you go through these portals, so ensure that you don't have to repeat your journey.

Look for the raised areas and, in some cases, beds on which you can rest and regain health, stamina and magic points without interruption by monsters. In the later dungeons, particularly the Imperial Palace, these safe zones are invaluable.

Night falls in Arena

COMBAT

Use the Shalidor's Mirror spell to get rid of monsters that fire at you. It is works especially well on wraiths, homunculi, hell hounds and stone golems. For the toughest monsters, such as fire daemons, vampires, medusae and liches, paralyze them immediately with a Force Bolt spell, then attack them with whatever spell or weapon you prefer like while they're immobile.

PASSWORDS

These are listed in no particular game play order: Sun, Rain, Shadow, Egg, E, Time, Footstep, Cell 2, Gauntlet/Glove, Air/Wind, Onion, 108, Theodorus, Key, Nothing, Hourglass, Match/Torch, Love, Water, Grape.

OUT OF THE IMPERIAL DUNGEONS

Exit the dungeon by following Ria's instructions (west, then south to the southwest corner); you must swim part of the way.

Rest on raised areas when possible.

Go to the Mages' Guild and buy spells and potions: get lots of Purification potions, which restore your health to maximum and make monsters ignore you as a target.

Also get proper armor and weapons, especially weapons or shields with magic protection.

Go to Chasetown, in Hammerfell province, and ask about Fang Lair: you will be sent to Rihad.

In the palace in the southeast corner of Rihad's map, talk to the Queen.

She will suggest going to Stonekeep to get a document for her, and will put Stonekeep on your map.

STONEKEEP

This is the fast way to explore Stonekeep:

When you enter the dungeon, save the game, then enter the first door on the left and collect the two treasures.

Go out the southern door and enter the left door, which leads to a room with four cells.

Get treasure from two of these cells, then go west through the door and west into a similar room with six cells

Get loot from one cell here, then go to the last cell on the north side.

Jump through the opening, swim west, kill the Ghouls, and get the document.

Return to the entrance and leave Stonekeep.

AN ALTERNATIVE WAY TO EXPLORE STONEKEEP:

Go south from the entrance to a small island in the center of a small lake.

Get the Iron Key on the island and use it to open up a few doors that access more parts of Stonekeep.

Go south to the King's bedroom until you find a note telling which way the King headed: this is the way to the document you need.

When you return from Stonekeep, visit Rihad's palace, and the ruler will put Fang Lair on your map.

FANG LAIR: STAFF PIECE #1

The entrance to Level 2 is in the southwest, and Fang Lair's entrance is in the northeast.

Follow the tunnels in a southwest pattern, remembering that the tracks always end at a mine pit.

You can see a vague outline, but always head south and west. (You may have to go north or east a short distance, but get back on the track as soon as possible.)

After descending a ladder to Level 2, you must defeat three skeletons to the north, then go east to a large room full of lava.

Fortify yourself with the Resist Fire spell and have a Purification potion ready.

In the center of the lava lake, there is a room with the door on the north side.

Open the door, slay the hell hounds and get Staff Piece #1.

Return to Rihad.

The first time you rest, Ria will send you to the Mages' Guild in Winterhold in the province of Skyrim.

You will be asked to make a trip to the Fortress of Ice to retrieve a tablet, and the location of the Fortress will be marked on your map.

67

FORTRESS OF ICE

You will use the password "Sun" here. Against Ice Golems, use a Frost Attack weapon or Purification potion, then move away and use a Fire weapon or spell from a distance. Be sure and use a Resist Cold spell on yourself.

As you enter the Fortress of Ice, note the blue square to the west on the map: this is the entrance to Level 2.

Just north of this spot, turn, face west and use the Passwall spell to make a clear path to the Level 2 entrance.

Descend the stairs.

FORTRESS OF ICE: LEVEL 2

You begin on the east side and must get the tablet for the Mages Guild on the northwest side by working your way south, west and north.

Use Purification potions to distract the knights you encounter, then slay them.

When you see a golem across a tunnel that you have to jump across, cast Lightning or Fire spells to melt him down.

You will also find underground tunnels and water that allow you to pass from room to room or over great areas in most of the Fortress level.

After you return to the Mages' Guild with the tablet, the Mage will indicate the location of the Labyrinthian on your map.

LABYRINTHIAN: STAFF PIECE #2

Passwords used here are: Air, Hourglass, and Key.

The Labyrinthian consists of a main room and two downstairs entrances that lead to east and west second levels, known as the lands of Kannin and Marcus.

On the second level, accessed by the western entrance, you need a key found in a cell in the southwest section of the dungeon; you must travel through many tunnels. Save before opening any door; if an Iron Golem lurks behind one, restore the saved position, magically seal the door and be on your way. Alternatively, you can kill him with a Purification spell as protection and a good sword.

On the eastern side, you need a key from the northeast corner.

After getting both keys, use them on the main level to enter the vault and get Staff Piece #2.

The next time you rest, Ria will tell you to go to Eldenroot and speak with the Queen, who wants you to go to recover Selene's heart.

SELENE'S WEB

From the entrance, go south and then west around a wall.

Next go north, then west along a long hallway and go south.

Take the first tunnel west and go south at the next opportunity.

You should now see the blue square that indicates the entrance to Level 2 on your map.

Cast an Open spell on the door; if this doesn't work, get the gold key from the eastern part of the dungeon just south of the long hallway.

SELENE'S WEB: LEVEL 2

You begin in a room containing tunnel entrances.

Enter the small hole in the southeast corner and follow the tunnel south, west and then immediately south again to enter a long hallway that ends at a diamond door toward the east.

Cast an Open spell to enter the diamond door, or use the key from the southeast area of this level.

Get the gem and return it to the Queen, who will place Elden Grove on your map.

ELDEN GROVE: STAFF PIECE #3

Due to the heavy fog, precise directions are impossible, so just work your way all the way into the southeast corner until you see a stone building, the entrance to Level 2. (You cannot use the Passwall spell on the brambles in the grove.)

To escape the cell on Level 2, use the password "Time."

Head west as far as you can go.

Levitate and go north.

Stop on a small island almost as far north as you can see on the map.

Use Purification, any spell that protects against other magic, and an Invisibility spell.

If you cannot answer the riddle at the door, cast Passwall to the left of the door and save the game.

Defeat the two wraiths, get Staff Piece #3 and some loot, then return to Eldenroot.

When you rest, you'll get a visit from Ria, who will send you to Corinth and the Halls of Colossus. See the Mage in the Mages' Guild and he will ask you to get an item from the Temple of Agamanus. After you retrieve his article, he will use it to locate the Halls of Colossus. In Corinth, you can buy a Buckler of Regeneration from Essential Provisions. Do so if you can afford it.

TEMPLE OF AGAMANUS

Go south until you reach a large four-way intersection. Go west through a door, then due south through another door and then south out of this room.

Head south in the hall, go west at the wall, then south to the stairs down to Level 2.

On Level 2, go north, then east and then south through a small maze until you reach the long vertical hallway in the center of your map.

Head east through two doors at the north end of the hallway.

Move north, then west through a door that leads down a path to the entrance to Level 3.

On level 3, go through the door on the east side. Continue south and enter the first door to the east. Levitate over the lava and go west through a door.

Fly west and then south over water to the southwest corner, then go north to your objective.

HALLS OF COLOSSUS: STAFF PIECE #4

Near the entrance to the Halls of Colossus, you'll find a dead man with a note about six keys that open a succession of doors on Level 2 and all other doors in the Halls of Colossus.

One key is due north in the northeast corner.

Another key is in the northwest corner of Level 1.

Go west, fly over a chasm and get the key here.

Now go south, then west from the entrance to find another key.

The other three keys are in the center, southeast and southwest areas of the map.

Descend the ladder on the east side, and you will find a large room with eight doorways out (including the ladder).

You may these doors to enter different areas of the dungeon.

If you enter Level 2 early enough, you will find that the keys you need are all near a doorway up from this Level.

THE KEYS & STAFF PIECE #4

You will need the passwords "Theodorus" and "108" here.

After passing through the five locked doors on the west side of Level 2 with the keys you've found, descend to Level 3.

Staff Piece #4 is in a large room protected by homunculi.

Cast a Shalidor's Mirror spell to kill the homunculi and protect you from their blasts.

After returning from the Halls of Colossus, you again receive a visit from Ria who tells you about the Crystal Tower (site of Staff Piece #5).

Lillandril in Summurset Isle is where you can get the location of the Crystal Tower.

See the Mage in the Mages' Guild, who wants you to locate a gem stolen by the priests of the Temple of the Mad God.

The Mage will inscribe the location of the Temple on your map, and the location of the Crystal Tower when you return the gem.

TEMPLE OF THE MAD GOD

After entering the Temple, go directly south, jumping two water squares.

Go through the west door, then south until the hall narrows.

Continue south through the door, then move directly west through a door and go west through another door into a room.

Go west into the room, then south.

Move west at the first opening, then go south through a door to the stairs leading down to Level 2.

On Level 2, head south through a door and go to the west and north through another door.

Move directly east through a door, then go north past a right and left passage.

Take the next east, next north, next east and go north, east and north into a room.

Move north out of this room through two doors to the gem, staying alert for a wraith.

Return to the Mages' Guild, and the Mage will show you the location of the Crystal Tower.

CRYSTAL TOWER: STAFF PIECE #5

You begin in the southwest corner and must work your way almost directly north of your starting location.

About halfway there, you will see the green dot on your map that marks the way up.

On Level 2, you begin in the northwest corner; the stairs up are in the northeast corner. Use Passwall just south of the steps.

LEVEL 3

Here you begin in the northeast corner and go west as far as the corridor that goes south, watching the west side of the wall for a large panel that will release all the cages.

Answer "Yes," then either continue south to the southeast corner (if you go this way, you will encounter some of the monsters you have turned loose), or go back to the entrance and use a tunnel near there, which goes south to a cell just north of where the fire daemon is caged.

You can also find a diamond key to open the locked door of the fire daemon's room after you kill a certain troll near the entrance to Level 3.

To slay the fire daemon, use your best weapon, Purification spell and Shalidor's Mirror spell.

After killing it, go up and you will be in the southeast corner of Level 4.

Work your way west until you see a large black wall.

You have to go south and to the west of this wall. Go around to the top door and answer "Egg."

Be prepared to fight a wraith inside.

Staff Piece #5 is in the center of the room.

71

BACK TO THE CRYSTAL TOWER

On your way out, be prepared to fight a fire daemon at the same spot as before on Level 3.

To reach the stairs down, enter the cell north of the fire daemon's cell and jump in the tunnel.

Go all the way north, use Passwall to get to the steps down, then make your way back to the entrance to the Crystal Tower.

When you rest, Ria informs you that your next stop is the Crypt of Hearts in High Rock.

Go to Camlorn in High Rock and ask about the Crypt.

You will be sent to the Brotherhood of Seth temple, where a monk says he will reveal the location of the Crypt of Hearts in exchange for a document from the Mines of Khuras.

MINES OF KHURAS

You begin in the north-central area and must get to the next level via steps down in the center of the map.

On Level 2, the dead monk with the document is in a cell in the southeast of the map.

Look for a red door south and east, staying alert for numerous monsters, including hell hounds, stone golems, iron golems and wraiths.

After retrieving the document from the dead monk, return to the Brotherhood of Seth.

CRYPT OF HEARTS: STAFF PIECE #6

The stairs down to Level 2 are in the northwest corner.

On Level 2, go directly south by using the Passwall spell to make a shortcut.

The room that you will enter contains the steps down to Level 3.

On Level 3, go south, also by using Passwall, until you see the blue dot on your map that marks the way down to Level 4.

On Level 4, go east into a long passage, then use the Passwall spell again to go north into a large room.

Use the Shalidor's Mirror spell to safely pass the homunculi and stone golems, or simply cast an Invisibility spell so they will not even know you're there.

Staff Piece #6 is in the center of the room.

MURKWOOD MYSTERY

Ria does not seem to appear after your next rest, but the name Murkwood appears in your list of places you can ask about.

Go to Stormhold in Black Marsh and visit the Conclave of Baal, where the monk will direct you to the Vaults of Gemin to retrieve something, then inscribe the location of Murkwood on your map.

VAULTS OF GEMIN

The Vaults of Gemin is the largest dungeon and the most difficult to navigate.

From your origin in the north-central area, go south.

Take the first east corridor to its end, follow the south corridor to its end, then go through the west door and out the south door.

Take the first west, then go south around a large wall.

Head west, then go north to the stairs down.

LEVEL 2

Cast a Levitation spell to hover over the water, go west a little, and then go directly south along the water.

Watch out for the homunculi on the islands: cast a Shalidor's Mirror spell to reflect their attacks and protect yourself.

Watch for a large room on an island in the south central area of the map.

Answer "Onion" to enter.

Get the plate and return to the entrance to the Vaults.

Return to the Conclave of Baal, then head to Murkwood.

MURKWOOD: STAFF PIECE #7

Go north and walk around the outer wall.

From the entrance, which is in the north central area, go directly south to a maze of bramble walls. In the center of this maze are masonry walls.

Follow the masonry walls around until you locate the entrance to a building.

Stay alert for lots of medusae and humunculi, which means you are near the building.

When you locate the entrance, answer the riddle with "Love," enter and descend to the next level.

LEVEL 2

As you enter, you will find Staff Piece #7 directly in front of you.

The answer to the riddle is "Water."

Exit Murkwood, go out to the nearest town, sleep, and you will find a new word in your vocabulary: Dagoth-Ur.

BLACK GATE

Go to Ebonheart in the Morrowind province and talk to the king, who will send you to Black Gate to recover a hammer.

As you enter, go south through two doors, west through a door and west across a bridge.

Shortly after crossing, work your way south to a bridge running south.

Levitate to the west, then south along the river.

Stop at the first red door and go west through the door.

You can get through the wall by casting Passwall to the west.

When you go through the wall, you will be at the stairs going down to Level 2.

LEVEL 2: GETTING THE HAMMER

On Level 2, answer "Rain" to get through the door blocking your way as soon as you enter the level.

Go south to three doors.

You must find one of three keys that allows you to enter the room that holds the hammer.

The quickest path is to take the western door, go west and south until you encounter an iron golem.

After slaying the golem, you will find a sapphire key that opens the sapphire lock on the door directly behind the golem.

The hammer is lying on a block of stone in this room, but you will have to fight another iron golem, a fire daemon and a vampire to get to it.

Take the hammer to the King in Ebonheart, and the Mount of Dagoth-Ur will appear on your map.

Stock up on Restore Power, Heal True and Purification potions in Ebonheart before you tackle the Mount.

MOUNT OF DAGOTH-UR: STAFF PIECE #8

When you enter, go west, then south to the first door on the west.

Go through the next door west, then proceed west on the path through the lava.

At the end of the path, go north.

Now go through the door to the west.

Levitate and move southwest to an opening.

Go west through the door ahead, then south to a large opening.

From here, head west, then southwest to a door on the southwest. (A vampire lives in this area. Avoid him if you can. He has a mithril key on him that will open the southwest door.)

Go south down the hall through the door, head to another door and take steps down to Level 2.

LEVEL 2

On Level 2, go north past a series of five doors that require different keys to open.

You can find the keys scattered throughout the level or, just south of the fifth door, use the Passwall spell to open the wall from east to west.

Use the diamond key to open the door to the steps down.

To get it, go north and follow the corridor around to the east and south to a maze of tunnels.

Crawl through them and enter the last tunnel at the south of the room.

You will go south, west, south, east, south and west through the tunnel.

As you come to an intersection, go south again and you will encounter your first lich.

THE LICH

Be sure you have full Health and Magic points.

Cast a Force Bolt spell to paralyze the lich, then use whatever means (weapon or magic) to take down its hit points.

Unlike vampires and trolls, liches disappear when you kill them.

The diamond key is behind the lich.

Get it and return to the door with the diamond lock. Open it and enter the stairs down to the Level 3.

LEVEL 3

Follow the hall to a huge lake of lava.

In the center of the lake is a building.

Fly there and save the game.

Enter one of the four doors by casting an Open spell, or jump over the wall.

Get Staff Piece #8 and answer the riddle with "E" to escape.

Go to the Imperial City in the Imperial Province.

IMPERIAL CITY

In the Imperial City, you must enter and survive the palace to find the gem that will completely defeat Jagar Tharn after you fight him.

From the entrance, head directly for the stairs down in the northeast corner.

Use a Shalidor's Mirror spell to breeze by the wraiths and homunculi.

On Level 2, find the stairs down near the southeast corner.

You will have to fight a variety of monsters and one vampire to get there.

On Level 3, the stairs down are on the west side of the level.

Work your way to the southwest corner, then north along the west side.

You should encounter only one vampire when using this route to get to Level 4.

LEVEL 4

Go north around the large room, then east, south and west to the entrance to the lava lake.

You will have to fight a large number of liches along this route — they are unavoidable.

Use the Force Bolt spell to paralyze them, then whatever method you desire to finish them off.

Enter the room and Levitate to reach the large platform near the center, where you will find four rooms and Jagar Tharn.

Fight Jagar Tharn: he is not much more powerful than a lich, but the Force Bolt paralyzation method lasts a shorter amount of time than with liches or other monsters.

Enter the northwest room and get the mithril key.

Go east and enter the northeast room with the key.

Click on the large ball to end the game.

After the animated sequences that conclude the story and major quest, you then find yourself back in the Imperial City, where you can continue to play the game and develop your character at will throughout the entire continent.

ORBS & STUFF

Countless objects are scattered throughout *Arena*, most of which are used in the various side-quests. The following lists only those items necessary for solving the game's main quest.

Object	See this Section for Location	Also See Section(s)
Iron Key	Stonekeep	Location only
Staff Piece #1	Fang Lair	Location only
Staff Piece #2	Labyrinthian	Location only
Staff Piece #3	Elden Grove	Location only
Staff Piece #4	Hall of Colossus	Location only
Staff Piece #5	Crystal Tower	The Keys & Staff Piece #4
Staff Piece #6	Crypt of Hearts	Location only
Staff Piece #7	Murkwood: Level 2	Location only
Staff Piece #8	Mount of Dagoth-Ur: Level 3	Location only
Tablet	Fortress of Ice: Level 2	Fang Lair
Buckler of Regeneration	Elden Grove	Location only
Hammer	Black Gate	Location only

GOBLINS QUEST 3

BY
FRED PHILIPP &
CLANCY SHAFFER

TYPE
Animated Adventure

SYSTEM
IBM & IBM CD-ROM (Required: 386/16+ MHz, 2 MB RAM, VGA, mouse, hard disk, sound card with DAC. Supports: SoundBlaster & Pro, Pro Audio, CD audio. Recommended: mouse)

COMPANY
Coktel Vision/Sierra

ANYONE WHO PLAYED THE FIRST GOBLIN GAMES KNOWS THE HARDEST PART WAS NOT FIGURING OUT THE ANSWERS TO THE PUZZLES, BUT MANIPULATING THOSE PESKY GOBLINS TO DO YOUR BIDDING. THIS DRAWBACK WAS ADDRESSED BY REDUCING THE NUMBER OF GOBLINS TO ONE, SO YOU NO LONGER HAVE TO DIRECT ONE CHARACTER TO PERFORM AN ACTION, THEN MADLY MOVE THE CURSOR ACROSS THE SCREEN TO BARK ORDERS AT ANOTHER ONE BEFORE TIME RUNS OUT. ASIDE FROM THIS WELCOME CHANGE, GOBLINS QUEST 3 RARELY STRAYS FROM THE DESIGN OF THE FIRST TWO GAMES.

AS A "GOBLIN REPORTER," YOU BEGIN THIS OFFBEAT JOURNEY ON A SHIP SAILING ABOVE THE CLOUDS, WITH THE GOAL OF INTERVIEWING THE INHABITANTS OF RIVAL TRIBES DWELLING IN THE LABYRINTH AND ULTIMATELY RESCUING A PRINCESS. INSTEAD OF WANDERING FROM

LOCATION TO LOCATION, YOU REMAIN IN EACH "PUZZLE AREA" UNTIL THE PROBLEM THERE IS SOLVED. ON-LINE HINTS AND A MAP ARE HELPFUL, AND IF YOU GET SERIOUSLY STUCK, YOU CAN USE ONE OF FOUR JOKERS: THE PROGRAMS DISPLAYS A SCROLL EXPLAINING STEP-BY-STEP HOW TO EVERY PUZZLE IN THE CURRENT SITUATION. IMMINENTLY MORE PLAYABLE THAN THE PREVIOUS GOBLIN GAMES, GOBLIN'S QUEST 3 PRESENTS A FRIVOLOUS COLLECTION OF PUZZLES THAT ARE AS ENTERTAINING AS THEY ARE CHALLENGING. THESE ARE A DISTINCT SET OF GAMES THAT ENJOY THEIR OWN SPECIAL NICHE IN THE WORLD OF ADVENTURE.

THE SOLUTION

VESSEL

PARROT

Untie the knotted rope on the top deck.

Hit the parrot with the golf club.

Use the coin to unscrew the hook by the doorway.

Get hook and attach to loop.

Open toolbox and get pepper and plunger.

Use plunger on Chump.

Put Blount by hook.

Use Chump on weight.

Have Blount take umbrella.

TOOTH

Put Blount on right hand at front of ship.

Put Chump on spring board at front corner of boat.

Have Blount get tooth.

Put Blount in barrel and put umbrella in hole in barrel.

Cut rope with tooth.

Looking for a hand near the Idol

....

IDOL

GUARDS

Use umbrella on hot air hole, then click on crevice to look at Wynnona.

Hit Hercules and Gromelon with the golf club.

Pick up the toast.

Use coin on Mac.

When Mac picks up coin, hit him with club.

WYNNONA

Put piece of toast in helmet and crush to crumbs with club; get crumbs.

Use springy stone by Idol to bounce behind Banzia.

Put crumbs in Banzia's collar, and when he squirms, hit him with the club and pick up his shield.

Use stone hand on Kendo, and while he is distracted, hit him with the club.

Put shield on branch by Zembla.

Go behind Zembla and use the pepper on him.

Pick up wooden club.

Use Chump to distract Django.

When guard sticks out his tongue, have Blount grab it.

Use wooden club on ladder.

Put Blount up ladder behind stone.

Have Chump distract Punky.

When he moves one step forward, have Blount push the stone.

DEATH

DARKNESS

Find the matches and strike them on the rough surface toward the top center of screen.

Get piece of scythe.

Free three wisps by using scythe on dens (the little holes in the wall).

BLUE WISP

Cut clown's water tube with scythe.

Take spectacles from clown's pocket and put them on skull.

Open top of skull.

When the blue wisp enters, close skull.

Open skull to get blue wisp.

YELLOW WISP

Set Pirate's wooden leg on fire with matches.

Put fire out with water from tube.

Get yellow wisp and put in bowl.

Press button near blood inscription and get mirror.

Put blue wisp in bowl.

When screen turns green, get cork from the hand.

Use mirror on green hand.

RED WISP

Use ladle on inscription to get blood.

Pour blood in bottle Pirate is holding, then get bottle.

Use blood on pedestal.

Use cork on bottle.

Remove blue wisp and yellow wisp with ladle.

Put red wisp in bowl.

When screen turns red, hit vampire's head with scythe.

Put blue wisp in bowl.

When screen turns purple, put spectacles on ghost skull.

Put yellow wisp in bowl.

COUNTRYSIDE

CASTLE

Pick up dolmen, then get the stone at left side of castle.

Take haystack and plunge into water basin.

Get sponge and use on fire.

Take pitchfork.

Put Chump on lever.

Have Blount use stone hand on meat.

Put Blount on lever.

Have Chump jump down.

Talk to king.

Open castle roof and talk to princess.

Jump down and use pitchfork on meat.

Put dolmen on thorns blocking Knight's way.

Talk to Knight, who will give you memorum potion.

Pour potion into basin.

Go to Inn at right of screen.

INN

Get spoon and put it on stone near exit to Countryside.

Enter crack in wall near Korin's sword.

Get sugar cube.

Click on coffee mug to get down.

Put Chump on spoon, then have Blount use sugar cube on end of spoon.

Put Blount beside Captain's right arm.

Use Chump on paprika, then use Blount to place meat under paprika cloud.

Return to Countryside.

DRAGON

Put gold coin in ear hole of den.

Put pitchfork in nostril hole.

Put spiced meat on pitchfork (you now have the dragon).

Retrieve the coin and return to the Inn.

INN AGAIN

Put Chump on right hand of customer and give the sugar cube to customer and get leash.

Use plunger on base of Othello's cage.

Use leash on plunger, then climb leash.

Give the coin to Othello, who will give you a key.

Use key to open door under cage.

Use dragon on open doorway to get lost note.

Get key, return it to Othello, get coin.

Talk to Captain and give him the note, and he will give you a message.

Give carved stone to Korin, then look at Korin's sword handle.

FORT & WYNNONA

DYNAMITE

Get gun powder at upper left.

Get hair off orange animal to use as fuse.

Pick up stick.

Use stick to reach flint behind Monk.

Ooya will appear.

Use flint on flute that Inca is holding.

Click on pipes that used to be the flute to place them.

Put pipe in hole.

Put powder, then put fuse in pipe.

Use flint on stone head to light dynamite stick. (You can blow up the beam and bricks this way.)

Use stick on skull to remove helmet, then get helmet.

Use flint on bark and put the glue in the helmet.

Make another stick of dynamite, but add glue to fuse before you light it.

Throw this on the door to explode it.

LARGE DYNAMITE

Put another pipe in place.

Use flint on pipe to create flute; give it to the Inca.

Put Ooya on gold tree stump.

When condor appears, have Ooya jump on it.

Use dynamite to blow up rock at bottom right, exposing bamboo shoot.

Use Ooya on bamboo shoot to make it grow.

Have Wynnona pick up bamboo.

Using bamboo to make large sticks of sticky dynamite, blow up the basement window, grate and wall.

When you run out of fuses, use Ooya on skull to grow hair and use it for a fuse.

After everything is blown up, talk to Fourbalus.

Wynnona will turn into a butterfly.

Have Blount use exit in middle of screen to go to town.

TOWN /LAB

TOWN

Talk to Nanny, then put umbrella in hole on roof.

Talk to Nanny again to get a hot water bottle.

Put hot water bottle on Boucassier egg to hatch.

SHOP

Enter shop and give coin to shopkeeper, then give him message from the Captain.

Get egg and key from left shelf.

Use key on moon lamp to turn Blount into Wolfy.

Use Wolfy on cupboard to throw it down.

Climb on cornice by moon lamp and jump on cupboard.

Take hammer from crack in cupboard.

Jump on sofa to produce spring.

Use spring to fling Wolfy up to shelf.

Use hammer on horn; get horn.

Use hammer on storage chest and get bird decoy from hole in chest.

Get spaghetti.

Go to the Lab.

LAB

Ring door bell twice, then enter.

Use left hand to read spell book.

Click on switch just left of spell book to turn the pages.

Make the Growixir potion.

Use right hand to pick up boa-boa egg and put on hot water bottle.

Crush eggshell in mortar with pestle.

Burn horn with a lighter in ashtray.

Use left hand to turn on faucet.

With right hand, use cup of water on kettle and put spaghetti in it.

Use lighter to light heater under pot.

Get cooked spaghetti.

Put all three ingredients in the mixer.

Press on/off switch with left hand to start the mixer.

Get the Growixir Potion.

Use potion on baby boa-boa to create Fulbert.

Make some more Growixir and pour into bottle on shelf.

GROWTH ELIXIR

In town, use potion on plant outside store.

Click on lever, put Blount on cannonball and use Fulbert on lever to send Blount to roof.

Have Fulbert climb plant outside store.

Use Fulbert across gap in roof to walk across.

Get shoe sole and enter chimney to get down.

Use potion to grow bud at foot of young woman.

SPEED ELIXIR

Have Fulbert climb stem so young woman will drop love letter.

Have Blount pick it up.

Have Fulbert climb stem again to loosen flower; grab it before it enters gutter.

Enter store and have Fulbert push button on shelf.

Have Wolfy use hammer on trap to get bone.

Have Wolfy lift night stand while Fulbert grabs soap underneath it.

Hit shopkeeper with hammer to retrieve coin.

Go to Lab.

Crush bone in mortar with pestle.

Fill kettle with water, put in sole and light stove.

Get boiled sole from pot.

Put flower in still and use lighter on burner.

Take essence of floriane, boiled sole and crushed bone and put in mixer.

Turn mixer on, get Speedixir and pour into bottle on shelf.

FAST FORWARD

In town, use the potion you just created on Blount to make him move fast.

Give baby Boucassier some Growixir.

Use Fulbert like a plank to get to the bell.

Use bird decoy on bell.

Position Fulbert over the gap, run and tap Boucassier's shoulders, then quickly run down and grab feather before it enters grate.

Put love letter in front of the mirror twice to see ingredients for Wingixir.

WING ELIXIR

Go to Lab.

Put memorum in still and light burner to get laughing tears of joy.

With lighter, burn the feather in ashtray.

Pour water into bowl on window sill, then add soap.

Turn on fan with coin.

Use key in soapy water, then use key on fan: a soap bubble will float into mixer.

Mix the three ingredients.

Pour potion into bottle.

———————   CLOUDS   ———————

OOYA

Pick up knife.

Use golf club on fishing thread to assemble fishing pole.

Talk to Ooya, then pull the cloud over the tuft of hair using the pole.

Exit screen to the southwest to go to Foliandre, and use the pole to get the telescope (by Colossus), then back to clouds.

Have Blount push air pump, and have Ooya grab it when it is within reach.

Have Ooya let go of balloon at next island.

Use Ooya on tuft of hair.

If Ooya should land on goat island or by exit, use him on rock to build a bridge back to Giant.

METEOROLOGIST

Put sandbag in basket of balloon.

Use knife on sandbag from ballast to knock out goat.

Blow up another balloon with pump, then hurry to the cloud.

Have Ooya grab balloon when it is within reach.

Use knife on cloud over Giant while Ooya is holding balloon.

When Giant sneezes, Ooya lands on island with geysers.

Put Ooya on upper geyser by anchor.

Use Blount to block lower geyser.

Ooya will be thrown to the next island.

Cut ballast from balloon until Ooya can enter it from upper ledge.

Add sandbags until Ooya can get off at glacier.

Use telescope on speck on glacier's island.

Use Ooya to defrost Bizoo and pick her up.

FOLIANDRE

Place Ooya on shovel and use button to swivel catapult to front.

Use telescope to activate catapult.

Ooya will land next to cheese.

Use Ooya on cheese to produce worm.

Walk Ooya to left.

Press catapult control button twice to center position.

Put Blount on shovel to land him on catapult.

Have Ooya push button once to turn catapult to right.

Use Ooya on ship painting above Colossus.

Blount should land next to cheese.

Have Blount use fishing pole on worm in cheese.

Go to Clouds and use pole on hole in clouds to get sawfish.

COLOSSUS

Press catapult button twice to get to center position.

Press loader control button once to get a rock on catapult.

Press control button twice to left position and fire it by using telescope.

A rock will knock off Colossus' helmet.

Put Bizoo on Colossus' face.

Enter mouth through loose tooth to get toothpick.

Put pick on eyelid, then look at eye.

Go through ear on left side of screen to remove grain of sand.

Pull on nose hair to get a tear from eye.

Throw grain of sand at tear.

Get toothpick.

Put Bizoo at top of scar in Colossus' beard.

Using toothpick, get rid of family of fleas in this order: Junior, Chubby, Meme, Gege, Mama and Papa. (If you are not fast enough, start over with Junior.)

Produce another tear by pulling nose hair.

Put Bizoo on it to cross the hair barrier.

Click on sand grain to kick it off.

GRAIN OF SAND (FACE)

Use sawfish to saw off base of right column holding hammock.

Use Ooya on Blount in cage to detach his shadow.

Have shadow pick up grain of sand.

Put grain in catapult gears and use Ooya on ship painting.

Pick up the gears that fly out of the machine.

Use knife to open robot by Fourbalus.

Put gears into hole in robot.

Take pollen expelled by robot.

Put pollen on Colossus.

Jump on nose.

When hand gets close to nose, walk back down to nose.

Get fleck of pollen from headband.

Put toothpick in nostril.

Put pollen in ear on right side of screen.

Jump on collar to push pollen through.

QUEEN/KING

QUEEN

Talk to Queen.

When her bodyguard appears, hit him with the hammer and take his gun.

Talk to Queen again.

She will kiss Wolfy.

When Mrs. Pyphie hides her eyes, take the wand.

Put Fulbert on plate on table.

Have Wolfy click on vegetables.

To reach fireplace, have Wolfy click on chandelier that is not moving.

Pick up fennel.

Have Wolfy and Fulbert go through door at far right and place Fulbert in front of bookcase at far left.

Move Wolfy up by bookcase.

Have Fulbert climb the colonnade.

While Wolfy is trying to get spectacles, quickly send Fulbert through the door to the flag-stone below to intercept spectacles.

Have Wolfy get spectacles and use them on onion.

Have Fulbert climb candle holder by Queen.

Have Wolfy get candle.

EXITING QUEEN'S THRONE ROOM

Put candle on one of three candelabras next to fountain.

Use wand on candle to light.

Blount's shadow appears and says portion of a sentence.

Move and light candle in this order to form a complete sentence: 2, 1, 3.

A mouth will open in the fountain.

Enter opening.

KING

THRONE ROOM

Talk to King.

Give hand to Bodd, gun to Tibo, and fennel to Rock Steady.

Use Fulbert on Rock Steady's spear to make light fixture swing.

To reach fireplace, have Blount click on fixture that is not swinging.

On the mantle, talk to Wynnona-butterfly.

Use onion on Iron Head.

When he cringes, get his axe.

Take dish from table.

Give wand to buffoon standing to right of King.

Use Fulbert on hole to left to King to make cockroach appear.

While King is hitting roach, give buffoon the dish.

Pick up the slipper before the guard with the spear gets it.

Talk to buffoon to get wand back.

Put out each candle in this order: 2, 3, 1.

Use coin on fountain mouth to cross fountain.

KING AND QUEEN

Give slipper to Queen, then use Fulbert on plate on table.

To reach fireplace, use Wolfy on vegetables, then on light that is not swinging.

Put axe in pot on mantle.

Move Fulbert to candle holder by Queen.

Hide Wolfy behind coat of arms.

When all the characters appear, send Fulbert up the candle holder.

The cook will throw the axe and cut the rope on the skull.

Get skull.

Go through fountain.

Give skull to Bodd and exit through door on left.

BIG BOOK ROOM

Enter Big Book room on right.

Use Fulbert on spider web while Wolfy sneaks past.

Use axe on wooden ruler to make blocks.

Pick up a block.

Take the horse.

Use Fulbert to kick up the dust, then move Wolfy under dust until he sneezes: numbers will fly.

Pick up all numbers except zero.

Place Wolfy at spider web and use Fulbert on the moon-lit scenery to take the number nine.

Get compass from sculpture book.

Draw the number eight by using compass on the piece of paper; get it.

Put all numbers except the zero into the ink bottle.

Dip ink brush into bottle.

Jump on geometry book three times.

Pick up the arrows.

Get chalk from drawing book.

THE BIG BOOK

Open Big Book and read it.

On the first page, use Wolfy on hole in tree, and an archer will appear.

To get Bowman, use arrows on hole.

Click on lower right corner to turn page.

On the next page, draw more of the path with ink brush.

Use Wolfy on tower.

Give horse to knight that emerges.

On the next page, draw a music player twice under window of house.

Get mandolin.

Put coin on wagon painting.

Draw a bull in front of the wagon.

Pick up coin.

Take a block of marble.

Return to chess board.

The Archer and Knight will be in position.

CHESS PIECES

Using right hand, draw outlines on wood and marble blocks with chalk on wood and compass on marble.

Use wood chisel with left hand and hammer with right hand to carve.

Get hammer with right hand.

Without putting hammer down, click on left hand and get the wood chisel.

Click on right hand and use hammer on wood chisel.

Complete Killer the same way with stone chisel.

Dip two pieces in paint.

Use ink brush to finish.

Put them on chess board.

CHESS GAME

Juggle balls with both hands.

Click on chess board.

Put coin in piggy bank: Othello emerges.

Play mandolin wrong-handed to hypnotize Othello: move the right hand to the mandolin fret board and move the left hand to the strings.

To scare off Chaperon, put Othello on blue square diagonally right of Chaperon.

CHESS MOVES

Move Knight to blue square between Killer and Lover.

Move Bowman one green square at a time to square below Knight's starting square.

The Bowman will shoot one of the Lancers.

Move Bowman to green square above so he can shoot other Lancer.

Move Bowman to green square in front of Hangman to shoot key off tower.

Move Lover one square at a time to the Chaperon's square and give him small mandolin by paint can.

Move Lover to key.

To get rid of Headsman, move Killer to square with lever.

Move Killer to axe (left) by the Headsman; he threatens King, who moves to the right and returns.

Move Killer to second blue square diagonally below.

Move Knight to square on right of King in three moves as follows: back to the original green square at far right, then to blue in exact middle, and finally to right of the King.

Move Bowman diagonally to tree stump square so his arrows cover the King's left escape square.

Move Killer to axe square.

HALL OF MIRRORS

Get egg and put in time mirror to hatch chick.

Put chick in fat mirror to fatten it.

Move Blount's reflection to upper passage.

Click on Blount and use chick on lower passage.

Select the reflection of Blount quickly, then click on chick.

Using Blount's reflection, click on big hole.

Using Blount's reflection, click on thinning mirror twice to make chick skinny.

Put chick back through passage for Blount.

To awaken Demon, use skinny chicken on small hole.

Click chick on fat mirror to return chick to normal.

Use baby chick on time mirror to turn it into chicken, then use chicken on fat mirror to get fat chicken.

Exit east to Brain.

BRAIN MAZE

Use Wolfy to break glass window on memory display in the upper center of screen.

To scroll through memories, use Blount to push exposed button.

When Colossus is displayed, use Wolfy on Colossus to knock out the grain of sand.

Have Blount pick up grain.

Use Wolfy to manipulate the lever on right side until the track above points to the lake.

Have Blount climb in the rail cart to land him on the Vision Lake shore.

Put Wolfy in the rail cart to land on the shore.

Have Wolfy jump in lake, then have Blount throw grain of sand in lake to produce a bubble.

Put Wolfy in cart so he sails through bubble to burst it.

Change track switch with Wolfy.

Put Wolfy in cart so he hits the suspended fish; the fish will take him for a ride to the other side of the screen.

Have Wolfy hit the wedged decoy on the wall, then go down the well and through the door.

Have Blount throw grain of sand in lake.

Send Blount down the red stone.

Have Wolfy go through the door and throw the switch to aim at the lake.

Put Blount in cart so he lands on bubble, bursting it.

Move Blount quickly to red stone.

Have Wolfy change track switch.

Put Blount in wagon and have him hit the suspended fish.

Have Blount pick up dragon decoy.

DRAGON DECOY

Send Blount down well and through door.

Use Growlixir on plant near window.

Create a step by having Fulbert climb the plant.

Have Blount go to the window and use dragon decoy on the window opening to call the dragon.

Give some Growlixir to the dragon.

Use decoy on the fence to have dragon burn it.

Move Blount through door near lake.

Use dragon decoy on the dream puddle to dry it up.

Pick up the key.

Send Blount through door and use key to open the box behind the fence and take the beauty ointment.

Have Blount ride the dragon to the grains.

Put fat chicken on the grains.

Pick up single piece of grain that remains.

Have Blount use the cart to return to the Hall of Mirrors.

REFLECTIONS

Throw folly grain of Madness on Old Demon.

Take the ointment of ugliness with Blount-reflection.

Move both Blount and his reflection to the Mirror of Beauty.

Move Blount close enough to see his reflection in the mirror.

Use ointment of beauty on mirror.

As soon as Blount becomes good looking, quickly switch to his reflection.

Use ugliness ointment on his reflection.

Both Blount and his reflection will exit automatically.

DEITIES

Talk to the Positive Pole to get the String of Time.

Break the wall at far right with hammer.

Break the fence at far left with axe.

Ring left doorbell, then quickly ring right doorbell.

While hands are stretched across holding chain, put Wolfy on chain.

Wolfy will bounce and knock the sacred score out of the god's hand.

Dump the sacred score in the spring.

Ring bell on left, then one on right.

Move to basin, and when it is empty, jump into the basin to recover the two scores.

SACRED SCORES

Put red score on the Demon's stand, and the yellow score on the Angel's stand.

Put coin in Angel's halo on ground.

Hit the cloud with the hammer to energize Demon's amplifier.

Throw the thread of time on the two notes that end up hovering above the basin.

Ring both bells as quickly as possible.

When the timing is correct, the hands will tie the thread of time and you will have restored harmony to the Kingdom!

ORBS & STUFF ▬▬▬▬▬▬▬▬▬▬▬

Because most objects in this quest are found in the area in which they are used, this table is structured differently from most. Each area's objects are listed together, with the precise location of the most important items that are not in open sight.

Object	See this Section for Location	Also See Section(s)

VESSEL

Object	See this Section for Location	Also See Section(s)
Golf club	deck	Parrot, Guard
Hook	by doorway	Parrot
Pepper	toolbox	Parrot, Wynnona
Plunger	toolbox	Inn Again
Tooth	by eyes	Colossus
Umbrella	hole in deck	Tooth, Guards, Town

IDOL

Crumbs	from toast	Wynnona
Stone hand	on ground	Wynnona, Castle
Helmet	Mac	Wynnona, Castle
Shield	Banzia	Wynnona
Toast	by Gromelon	Guards, Wynnona
Wooden club	Zembla	Wynnona

DEATH

Blood	inscription	Yellow Wisp, Red Wisp
Bottle	pirate	Red Wisp
Cork	green hand	Yellow Wisp, Red Wisp
Ladle	on bowl	Red Wisp
Matches	lower screen	Darkness, Yellow Wisp
Mirror	yellow button	Yellow Wisp, Fast Forward
Scythe	skeleton	Darkness, Blue Wisp, Red Wisp
Spectacles	clown	Blue Wisp, Red Wisp, Queen
Water tube	clown	Blue Wisp, Yellow Wisp

COUNTRY

Dolmen	grass	Castle

Haystack	by fire	Castle
Meat	mousetrap	Castle, Inn, Dragon
Memorum	knight	Castle, Wing Elixir
Pitchfork	by fire	Castle, Dragon
Stone	under dolmen	Castle, Inn, Inn Again

INN

Key	Othello	Inn Again, Shop, Wing Elixir, Chess Moves, Dragon Decoy
Leash	customer	Inn Again
Letter	captain	Speed Elixir, Fast Forward
Note	Othello's home	Inn Again, Sacred Scores
Paprika	top shelf	Inn
Spoon	carpet	Inn
Sugar cube	through crack	Inn, Inn Again

FORT/WYNNONA

Bamboo	under rock	Large Dynamite
Flint	by monk	Dynamite, Large Dynamite
Fuse	little animal, skull	Dynamite, Large Dynamite
Glue	stick bark	Dynamite
Gun powder	steps	Dynamite
Helmet	skull	Dynamite
Stick	by monk	Dynamite

TOWN

Feather	boucassier	Fast Forward, Wing Elixir
Floriane	bud	Speed Elixir
Water bottle	nanny	Town, Lab
Love letter	young lady	Speed Elixir, Fast Forward
Shoe sole	roof	Growth Elixir, Speed Elixir

SHOP

Boa-boa egg	shelf	Lab
Bone	trap	Speed Elixir
Bird decoy	storage cabinet	Shop, Fast Forward
Hammer	cupboard	Shop, Speed Elixir, Queen, Chess Pieces, Deities, Sacred Scores

99

Key	shelf	Shop
Soap	nightstand	Speed Elixir, Wing Elixir
Spaghetti	floor	Shop, Lab

CLOUDS

Fishing thread	ground	Ooya
Knife	ground	Ooya, Meterologist, Grain of Sand
Sandbag	by geyser	Meterologist
Sawfish	hole	Foliandre, Grain of Sand

COLOSSUS

Cheese	ledge	Foliandre
Gear	catapult	Grain of Sand
Pollen	robot	Grain of Sand
Telescope	by Colossus	Ooya, Meteorologist, Foliandre, Colossus
Worm	in cheese	Ooya, Foliandre, Colossus, Brain Maze

GRAIN OF SAND (FACE)

Sand	eye	Colossus, Grain of Sand, Brain Maze
Toothpick	mouth	Colossus, Grain of Sand

QUEEN

Candle	candlestick top	Queen, Exiting Queen's Room, King and Queen
Fennel	mantle	Queen, Throne Room
Gun	bodyguard	Queen, Throne Room
Onion	table	Queen, Throne Room
Skull	column	King and Queen
Spectacles	book case	Queen
Wand	Mrs. Pythie	Queen, Exiting Queen's Room, Throne Room

KING

Axe	Iron Head	Throne Room, King and Queen, Big Book Room, Chess Pieces, Deities
Dish	table	Throne Room

HEXX: HERESY OF THE WIZARD

BY
CLANCY SHAFFER
& FRED PHILIPP

TYPE
Fantasy Role-playing

SYSTEM
*IBM
(Required:
386/20+, 800
free EMS,
256-color
VGA/MCGA,
Microsoft-
compatible
mouse.
Supports:
Sound
Blaster, Ad
Lib, Roland
LAPC &
SCC1, Gravis
Ultra)*

COMPANY
Psygnosis

N THIS EUROPEAN IMPORT, YOU DIRECT THE ACTIONS OF A QUARTET OF ADVENTURERS ON A QUEST TO DISCOVER FOUR MAGIC GEMS AND REPLACE THEM IN A TOWER. THE QUEST IS LENGTHY, CONSISTING OF EXPLORING MAZES WHERE YOU PUSH BUTTONS TO ALTER THE STRUCTURE AND OPEN NEW DOORS OR REMOVE BLOCKED PASSAGES. THESE FEATS ARE ACCOMPLISHED BY FINDING KEYS, UNLOCKING DOORS, AND PUSHING BUTTONS TO GET INTO THE NEXT AREA — WHERE YOU START LOOKING FOR MORE KEYS. UNLIKE MOST AMERICAN GAMES, *HEXX* DOES NOT EMPLOY FIRST-PERSON GRAPHICS THAT SHOW THE MAZE THROUGH THE EYES OF YOUR PARTY. INSTEAD, YOU SEE AN ISOMETRIC VIEW THAT DEPICTS THEM FROM OVERHEAD VIEW AT AN OBLIQUE ANGLE. AN AUTO-MAP HELPS SIGNIFICANTLY, AND THE REGENERATION CHAMBER FOR REVIVING DEAD CHARACTERS WILL SEE LOTS OF USE. A NOVEL "RESTORE GAME" FEATURE SHOWS A PICTURE OF THE SCENE

WHERE YOU SAVED EACH GAME, MAKING IT EASIER TO LOAD THE ONE YOU WANT. WHILE THE MAGIC SPELLS AND COMBAT CAN BE FUN, THE REPETITIVE NATURE OF THE "PUZZLES," WHICH CONSIST MAINLY OF FINDING KEYS AND PUSHING BUTTONS, PUT A HEX ON *HEXX*'S CHANCE OF GETTING MORE THAN A NOD FROM THIS REVIEWER.

THE SOLUTION ▬▬▬▬▬▬▬▬▬

GENERAL

In most instances you carry only one key at a time, so you know what to do next: find the door that the key you are carrying will unlock.

To progress through each level, push all the buttons and pull all levers you find, then check your map to see what has changed: you will usually see that a path or wall has been opened, or an obstacle has been moved out of your way.

CHARACTERS & GEAR

Use two Mages: Mad Meg, who has Confuse from the outset, and later can cast Wychwind and Mindrage, and Zothen Runecaster, who can cast Damage.

You also need Two Warriors up front to keep the monsters away from the Mages.

Get a bow and arrows for the rear characters, who can do real damage with the Hail of Doom-type arrows from a Harvester bow (with Archer skill the damage is about 450).

Swords range from a short sword to a Rune sword, and the battle Staff can be wielded from the rear rank; the best armor is Crystal Plate.

There are a number of Magic rings, staffs and wands, but you will need a Recharge spell to regenerate them after about seven uses. But if you sell them to a shop and repurchase them, they will be fully charged.

There is a Regeneration Chamber in the southwest section of Level 6, where you start; a bed is in the lower left center.

There are also two shops on this level, selling armor, weapons, food, scrolls and potions.

HELPFUL HINTS

Sleeping in beds will restore Hit Points and Magic Points to the maximum, and also gives you an opportunity to buy magic spells.

Regeneration Chambers will return your Hit Points to the maximum, but not your Magic

Points.

Shops sell armor, weapons, food, torches, rings, amulets, potions and spells (there are no Shops outside of the Keep, so stock up on lots of food and torches before leaving the Keep to enter the structures.

Alternatively, you can use the Torch spell (if you have it) to provide light.

TRAVELLING & KEYS

Backpacks will hold up to twelve items, but only count as one item in your inventory slots.

Each Monster you slay will drop a bag of gold and sometimes a key; you must also buy or find "Common Keys" to unlock "Common Doors".

Pile common keys together to save space.

Throughout this quest you will constantly be going up a level, then down, then up, then down, and so on. The important thing is to cover all areas on all Levels in your search for keys. Consult your map frequently.

THE KEEP

You begin in the Keep on Level 6, where the initial objective is to reach the center of this level and find four Teleport Pads, which will transport you to other areas of this level, including the stairs down to Level 5.

Eventually you must progress down to Level 1 and back up to Level 6, until you have mapped all areas except for two: in the northwest corner of Level 6 is a room with four openings in the wall, where you will place the artifacts you acquire.

The other area you will not have yet mapped is on Level 4, where you will encounter four locked gates leading to the four main structures that you must enter in order to obtain the four artifacts necessary to completing the game.

Mapping all of the Keep in this linear manner will eventually result in the acquisition of a key that unlocks the gate to the first of these structures, the one to the north, which leads to Grisslem's Tower.

LEVEL SIX

Look at your automap and explore this level until all five switches appear on the map:

Switch 1 is to the north.

Switch 2 is in the southeast, facing a column that bars your path.

Switch 3 is in the southeast.

Switch 4 is in the middle western side of the map.

Switch 5 is south of Switch 4.

Go north to Switch 1 (watch out for the teleportal just north) and pull the red switch.

This causes the column in the southeast to face north.

Go to Switch 5 and push the gray button, which removes the column and allows access to Switch 2.

Push the green button, which rotates Switch 4.

Go to Switch 3 and pull the red lever, which allows you to reach Switch 4.

Pull the green lever.

Go west to the teleport pad, which takes you north to the Ruby Key.

Step back on the pad to leave the area.

Go northeast opposite the shop, use the Ruby Key and get the Sun key.

LEVEL FIVE

Go to Level 5 and through the west door.

Go down the Hall and get a Crystal Key.

To deal with the monsters just released, run down the hall and exit, then turn and fight them (close the door if you need some time to heal).

As you work your way down, you will have to move back and forth between floors to make progress; watch out for Spinners.

THE GEMS

After you get each Gem, return to Level 6 and place it in a pocket.

This opens a door further west and allows you to proceed to another Tower.

On the last trip, take all four Gems back to the Wizard's Tower.

The Eye doubles your strength while being carried and renews the entire party when placed in the wall.

The Tear doubles dexterity and restores magic points.

The Heart doubles constitution and restores vitality.

The Horn doubles intelligence and Vivifies the party.

STONEWALLED

To get past the stone wall on Level 6, you must find a key on Level 5, which will open the rest of Level 6's northwest section.

Next work your way to Level 1, then back up to Level 5 and open the stairway to Level 6.

Go back down to Level 4, then go north to the entrance to the Tower of Grisslem.

THE TOWER OF GRISSLEM

Start up the east stairs of this eight-level tower.

Get the Eye from the north-central wall on Level 8.

Go back down to Level 7 and drop down into the pit to reach Level 6 (there is a regeneration chamber on this floor).

Look for a blue button in the southeast corner, then use the steps from Level 6 to reach Level 5.

Descend to Level 4 by going north via the spinner.

Go east and south, then enter the south pit to reach Level 3 (a pit in the south on Level 3 will take you to Level 1).

Use the teleportal to return to Level 4 of the Keep.

Go to the southeast corner and take the steps to Level 5.

Go to Level 6, then head west and put the Eye in the proper hole, which will open a door to the west.

Take the door to the south, and you will find a key that opens the next tower.

Go south on Level 4, open the door with the night key and use the teleportal in the south to reach the Demesne of Shaspouk.

THE DEMESNE OF SHASPOUK

Go south and up to Level 2 (you'll find an Armorer and a magic shop on this level).

Visit every part of Level 2, then go north and use the west hall to get to the stairs on Level 3.

On Level 3, cover every square foot completely, then go to the southeast corner and take the two sets of stairs to Level 4.

On Level 4, a spinner teleports you back to where you started: when you go north, try to move to one tile away from the north wall.

When you see a sign, run the Gauntlet: use the pads one at a time and kill each monster as it appears.

In the south alcove, press button one (between the second and third projection) to open the east door and reach the stairs to Level 5 (there is a Regeneration Chamber on Level 5).

The stairs up are in a room in the northeast area: cover the whole floor for keys.

On Level 6, explore the floor, then take the stairs in the southeast quadrant to Level 7.

Using the Night Key from Level 6, go to the northeast corner and push the blue button behind the fake wall.

Go to the southwest corner and go through another fake wall, then go west, north and east and get the Tear.

Use the steps down to Level 6, and go to Level 5 via the pit in the central-east room.

Take the steps to Level 4, then go around west and north, then south to the stairs that lead to Level 3.

Use the pit in the center to reach Level 2, and take the steps to Level 1.

Teleport back to Level 6 of the Keep and place the Tear in the slot.

Go west and south to get the Ruby Key.

Go to Level 4, use the Ruby Key in the south room and use the teleport to get to the Citadel of Angrath.

THE CITADEL OF ANGRATH

Take the steps to Level 2, a tough level with numerous fake walls and spinners.

Cover the entire floor, get the Ruby Key from the center room, then go to the northwest quadrant and use the key on the west side to get to the stairs that lead to Level 3.

On Level 3, get the Gold Key that opens the southwest corner and leads to the stairs up.

On Level 4, get the Ruby Key in the small north-central room.

With the Ruby Key, go north, west and south to reach the stairs to Level 5.

On Level 5, use Antimage to counteract the Arcbolts; some squares here will remove your spell, so you can die often.

Find the safe squares (save the game when you discover one), recast the spell and heal yourselves, then move on.

Go to the northwest, then east and south for the stairs to Level 6.

On Level 6, the stairs up are in the northwest.

In the center of Level 7 are two sets of stairs on the left and right: use either one.

On Level 8, use the Ruby Key to get the Heart.

Return to Level 1, use the teleport on 2, then return to Level 6 and put the Heart in its slot.

Go west for the Sun key, which opens the Tower of Xtlaltic.

Meet the party in Hexx.

....

THE TOWER OF XTLALTIC

....

Use the Sun Key to enter and clear out the south room, then use the teleport to Level 1.

Now work your way up to Level 7, in search of the Horn.

On Level 2 you will need Levitate spells; also watch out for spinners.

You'll find a shop and a Regeneration Chamber on Level 2.

Move to the southwest to take the stairs up to Level 3, where you will need a Sun Key.

Go south and west to the stairs up to Level 4, then on to Level 5.

Return to Level 4 via the pit, take another pit back to Level 3, then another pit to Level 2 and back up to Level 5 and Level 6.

Save the game.

Drop down into the pit.

Cast Levitate, and while passing a green button, press it (this removes a column to the north on Level 4).

Go north to Level 4 and get the Ruby Key.

Go down the pit to Level 3, cancel Levitate and go south to the steps down to Level 2 (you can also find a good weapon north of here).

Go back to Level 5 via the southwest steps and go down the pit to Level 4.

Go north and down the pit to Level 3.

Save the game.

THE HORN

On Level 3, go to the northwest room and move up and down levels between this room and one in the northwest on the Level 6.

Save the game, then use the left teleport pad to go up to Level 6.

Step on the pad in front of the blue button, step off and back on again, push the blue button and step off again.

Push red button and step to the teleport pad in back, which transports you to Level 3.

Use the right teleport pad again to reach Level 6, then push the green button and go to the rear teleport pad, Level 3.

Step on the left teleport pad and go to Level 6.

Push the green button and use the rear pad on Level 3.

Use the right teleport (Level 6), then press the red button and get the Night Key out of the room in back of you.

Step on the pad in front of the blue button, step off, then step on and off again.

Step on the rear teleport pad to reach Level 3, then step on the center teleport pad and teleport to the exit hall.

Press the blue button to create a second blue button; press this, and you are arrive on Level 6.

Go to Level 5 and use the pit to reach Level 4.

Use the pits or stairs to reach Level 2.

THE HORN AT LAST

Go up the stairs to Level 3 and use the Sun Key.

Finish visiting every part of this level (take the steps down in the northeast area to completely finish it, particularly the southeast part).

Then use the stairs to reach Level 4.

Explore Level 4, noting the pit in the northwest, which you will use later.

Go northeast and take the stairs to Level 5, which is filled with spinners on this floor.

Find the Ruby Key, then go south of it for the Night key.

Go south through a fake wall and use the Ruby Key on the door.

Move east to a pad on front of a door; the pad rotates the door.

Step on the pad, then off and on, until you are able to go west through the door.

Then go south and east to another pad, which revolves the door you just came through: stand on it until you can go south.

Return to this door and get the Sun Key, then use it to the north and get the Gold Key.

Go to the second pad, near the southeast corner, and stand on it three times, so that the room where you got Sun Key revolves from to south to west access.

Use the Gold Key on the west door, and you'll find stairs to Level 6.

On Level 6, you must go to the northeast corner to find stairs to Level 7.

Go south and drop through a pit to Level 6.

Go south on Level 6 through two doors, then east and get the Sun and Silver Keys.

Use the Silver Key to open a door to the southeast, and again go up to Level 7.

Just west of the stairs is a Sun Key, and to the west, a yellow button.

Press the yellow button to remove a pillar to the north, then go there and use the Sun Key.

Press the yellow button to the east.

Use the second Sun Key to open a door to the northwest room, then press the yellow button there (this opens the door to the center).

Return to the back of the column and press yet another yellow button, which removes a teleport pad from in front of the Horn.

Take the Horn.

INTO THE WIZARD'S TOWER

Descend into the pit on the west side to reach Level 6.

In the east part of the central area, enter the pit to Level 5.

Take the northeast stairs to Level 4.

In the northeast room on Level 4 are two pits: use the southern one to reach Level 3.

Take the south steps to Level 2, then the east steps to Level 1 (you must use the Crystal Key to get out).

Take the Horn to Level 6 and insert it into the slot, which opens the way to the Wizard's Tower.

Take all four items before leaving Level 6.

NONE SHALL PASS

Note the teleport pad you arrive on: if you want to leave the building you can do so at any time.

You must get to the southeast corner, then proceed north to reach the steps to Level 2.

In the center is a sign: "None shall pass."

Use the pit just to the south to finish up Level 1, then return by using the steps in the northwest.

Pull the red lever south of you, which gives access to the room in the center.

Open the west door with the Ruby Key.

Stand on the pad, and it will remove the pit you used before and replace it with a pad.

Standing on the new pad opens door to the east, where you must pull a red lever.

Move west and south, then go north to the stairs up to Level 3.

Go to the stairs in the north-central area of Level 3 to reach Level 5.

FOUR COLUMNS

On Level 5, find the Silver key and use it on the west door.

Continue west and open all doors (one leads to a healing chamber).

Go east, open the north door and slay anything that moves.

In the center are four columns: put the Tear in the south column.

Stay close to the walls and go east, where you will put the Heart, then go north and west to the west column and place the Horn in this column.

Open the door behind you, go north and place the Eye in the north column.

(You must place the items in the order described.)

When you place the Eye, it removes a column north of you: step on either pad here, and it will send you into the center room to fight the toughest monster of all.

If you need to escape and heal, stand on the west teleport pad, which creates a teleport pad to the west; standing on the west one creates a pad to the north; standing on the north one creates another to the south that will teleport you out.

When ready to leave, press the button in the northwest room.

You must kill the monster to finish the quest.

ORBS & STUFF ▬▬▬▬▬▬▬▬

Because the keys are found in such a linear manner that is noted in the solution, their locations are not listed here.

Object	See this Section for Location	Also See Section(s)
Eye	Tower of Grisslem	The Gems
Tear	The Demesne of Shaspouk	The Gems, Four Columns
Heart	The Citadel of Angrath	The Gems, Four Columns
Horn	The Horn	The Gems, The Tower of Xtlaltic, Into the Wizard's Tower, Four Columns

INCA 2

BY
FRED PHILIPP AND
CLANCY SHAFFER

TYPE
*Animated
Adventure,
limited space
combat*

SYSTEM
*IBM
(Required:
386DX25
MHz+, CD-
ROM, 4 MB
RAM, mouse,
hard disk.*

*Supports:
SoundBlaster,
ProAudio)*

COMPANY
*Coktel
Vision/Sierra*

F YOU FINISHED THE ORIGINAL *INCA*, YOU WILL PROBABLY WONDER HOW ELDORADO, THAT GAME'S CHIEF CHARACTER, MANAGED TO RETURN FROM THE DEAD TO PLAY A MAJOR ROLE IN *INCA II*. KEEP WONDERING, BECAUSE THAT'S JUST ONE OF THE STRANGE THINGS THAT GOES UNEXPLAINED IN THIS OFFBEAT BLEND OF ADVENTURE AND SIMULATION. AT THE OUTSET, YOU WITNESS THESE AND OTHER EVENTS THROUGH THE EYES OF ELDORADO'S SON, ATAHUALPA — AN INCA WITH AN ATTITUDE SO BAD, HE SETS OFF AN INTERSTELLAR WAR FASTER THAN YOU CAN SAY "FILE NOT FOUND." THIS IS WHERE THE SIMU-LATION SIDE OF *INCA 2* COMES IN: THE ADVENTURE IS INTERMITTENTLY INTERRUPTED BY SIMU-LATED SPACE COMBAT SCENES THAT YOU MUST FINISH TO GET BACK TO THE PUZZLE-SOLVING. AFTER ATAHUALPA GETS BLASTED INTO ATOMS, YOU ASSUME THE ROLE OF HIS SON, ELDORADO, AND SET OUT TO STOP A SERIES OF DISASTERS CAUSED BY A MYSTERIOUS ASTEROID.

THE "POINT AND QUEST" INTERFACE IS EASY TO USE WHEN EXPLORING AND SOLVING PUZ-

ZLES, BUT THE SPACE SHIP CONTROLS COULD PROVE FRUSTRATING FOR ANYONE UNACCUSTOMED

TO SIMULATIONS (AND EVEN SOME WHO ARE!). VIVID GRAPHICS AND A VARIETY OF SOUND

EFFECTS AND MUSIC ARE AMONG INCA II'S MAIN ATTRACTIONS, BUT THE LESS THAN LOGICAL

PUZZLES AND BIZARRE STORY PREVENT THE STORY AND ITS PRESENTATION FROM COALESCING IN

A COHESIVE FASHION — IN OTHER WORDS, IT'S JUST NOT AN EASY GAME TO "GET INTO," ONE

RECOMMENDED MAINLY FOR GAMERS WHO ENJOYED THE ORIGINAL *INCA*.

THE SOLUTION

GATE OF WISDOM

Take feather from guard's headdress.

Take stone from lower left side of screen.

Put stone in gutter to divert water to left side of statue, then use feather on statue.

Repeat same procedure on right statue to open both gates.

Walk through open gates.

GATE OF FORCE

This is an arcade sequence in which you shoot at statues. There are about 50 statues on the course, and you must shoot at least 26 to pass the test.

TUMI

Click on cocoa leaves and take the post with the rope attached.

Place post above gate entrance to right.

Return to pile of rocks and throw one at the guard above you on the ledge.

Quickly hide behind vegetation to your left, or hide behind the fence to your right.

When the guard walks to the entrance, click on the rope (so the post falls on the guard).

SPACE COMBAT: TACTICS

Stop the Tumi and use the weapons you have.

First use the Atomic Disintegration Bombs, then the Clean Nuclear Torpedoes.

Start your engines, accelerate, and pick off the remaining targets.

Hold off using your 1A Missiles until you are near the target.

Use your map to change targets. By selecting targets, the Tumi can dart to areas of battle and attack specific ships. Use these tips in future space battles.

CABIN

Click on the Control Panel.

Click on control keys and enter any three-digit number on your computer numeric keypad.

Enter the Airlock.

Scroll to the left and click on a portion of a pipe called a Reservoir.

Get the crowbar.

Scroll to the right and use the crowbar to pry open the case of vodka.

Get a bottle of vodka and return to the Reservoir.

Click on it and pour the vodka into it.

Exit the airlock and return to the Control Panel.

Click on it and choose either F1 or F2 for gun position.

Exit the Panel screen and click the throttle lever to the "on" position.

THE MAP

To plot on the map, click on the center of the waterhole left of the mountain range.

Go northeast about 160 miles and click near the tip (to the left of the dark green valley).

Go 100 miles southeast, past the mountain range and click in the center of the light green area between the large mountain range and the two smaller mountain peaks.

Go south 150 miles and click on the medium dark green area.

Go east 330 miles and click on the upper right tip of the water hole.

Move the Planet into center on display.

THE TRAIN

Enter the train and get oil.

Exit and use oil on the pulley under the water tower.

Get the crowbar and use on pulley.

Enter train and use crowbar on the peg.

Remove strap.

Open valve.

Turn ignition on.

One of the wacky Incas in Inca 2, a science
fiction-flavored pre-Columbian pot luck.

·····················

TRENCH COMBAT

During this arcade sequence you will see four red directional arrows.

When attack commences, a red arrow will start blinking.

Click on it to reach the location of the attack and another shoot 'em up scene.

THE CAVE

Click on the chest and take the bottle of Mercury, the light thread, mallet, key and shaver.

Use Mercury on safe dials to remove rust.

Go to file cabinet and cut rope with shaver.

Zoom in on the drawer and use the key on the sand to remove rust.

Unlock drawer with key and view the plans for the spaceship "Boomerang" inside.

Note numbers on plan (1, 8, 3).

Use this combination on safe and open it.

LEAVING YUNA

After conversing with Yuna (the female Astronomer at the Planetarium), you will leave her.

In the next scene, put the crystal in the memory socket to show planets.

Choose Planet A.

IBIS

Click on the broken stems left of the screen to enter the Mangrove.

Click on the palm leaf and use leaf on the ground to expose footprints.

Get oyster and throw it at the monkey. The monkey and Ibis will flee.

Get another oyster and put it on the rock.

Hit oyster with the mallet.

Zoom in and get the pearl.

Look at nest and click the pearl on the emerald egg.

You will return to the crocodile. Put the pearl and egg into the eye sockets of the crocodile to revive him.

CRATER

Scroll right and click near the bottom of the wall to see the door's outline.

Below the door are two scepters. Take them.

Enter door and use mallet on the gourd.

Get two gourd pieces.

Exit and return to pillar.

Scroll to the left and place one piece of gourd on the keystone above the cave entrance.

Return to pillar.

Insert two scepters and the remaining piece of gourd into blocks on the ground.

You will receive a gem. Place gem in the now-shattered sphere.

SPACE COMBAT IV

Say "no" at end of the first wave if you want to avoid further combat at this point.

CLIFF

Use peg on the block of stone and hit it with the mallet.

Scroll up one screen and click on ballast rope on rock.

Go back down and use light thread on end of rope.

Pull on light thread and attach the end of the rope to the peg.

Click on the small stones, then on the block of stone.

PRAYER SCROLLS

You need to click on the prayer scrolls so that all three prayers are in the air at the same time.

Clicking on an "even, even, odd" combination works. Use 2, 4, 7. You will receive a conch.

PLATEAU

Click on the opening and take chain.

Click chain on point at base of the lightning rod. Lightning will strike the rod and melt the chain.

Use crowbar on casting to get a shield.

AVALANCHE

Give the conch shell to the Lama.

Click on sticks located in snow to left of screen.

Click sticks on snow.

Put strap on sticks.

Put shield on strap.

Hit gong with mallet.

TEMPLE

Use mallet on icicles.

Pick up broken pieces and place them on the spot where the sun is shining. The ice will melt.

Quickly click on the waterskin and place it under the melting ice.

Pour the water into the basin.

THE NECKLACE

Get necklace from the guard.

Use shaver to cut cord.

Use crowbar on hatch located on left side of opening.

Insert pearls from necklace into correct shapes on the panel.

Use mallet on each pearl to fix in place.

Exit screen and click on opening.

Use mallet on ledge.

Return to panel and press all buttons. The key will light up, the panel will close and the pearls will fall out.

Get three pearls and return to the opening.

Get mallet.

Insert three pearls in appropriate hollows. (The game ends here in the floppy version.)

ROOMS MAZE: CD-ROM VERSION ONLY

Halfway through each tunnel you will encounter an eye.

Click on the eye to continue.

For now, go right, left, right, right, right.

Click on the eye to reach the Statues Room.

STATUES ROOM

Click on one of the statues to get a diamond.

Click on the tunnel.

Click on the eye.

Go right, left, right, right, right, left, left.

Click on the eye.

ROOM OF MIRRORS

Use the diamond to cut off a piece of the mirror.

Click on the tunnel, then on the eye.

Proceed right, right, right, left, right, right, right.

Click on the eye.

ROOM OF PICTURES

Use the cut piece of glass (from the mirror) on the picture of Atahualpa, Eldorado's son, to get a music box.

Return to the Room of Statues.

Click on the tunnel, then click on the eye.

Go left, left, right, right, right, left, right.

Click on the eye to enter the Room of Statues.

Click the music box on one of the Statues.

THE FLOWER PUZZLE

The object is to pollinate a flower to produce all three colors on one flower. Colors are blue, a reddish orange and green. The solution involves several steps:

1) click on a flower to open it.

2) Click on the Stone of Light icon on the flower petal to reveal its true color.

3) Click on the flower to get the pollen.

4) Go to the next flower and repeat steps 1 and 2. 5)

If the color is different from the first flower, then click the pollen from your inventory on the flower. Click on the flower again and use the Stone of Light to reveal two colors. Repeat steps 1, 2 and 5 to reveal three colors.

ORBS & STUFF

Object	See this Section for Location	Also See Section(s)
Feather	Gate of Wisdom	Location only
Stone	Gate of Wisdom	Location only
Cocoa leaves	Tumi	Location only
Rope	Tumi	The Cave, Cliff
Crowbar	Cabin	The Train, Plateau, The Necklace
Vodka	Cabin	Location only
Pulley	The Train	Location only
Peg	The Train	Cliff
Chest	The Cave	Location only
Mercury	The Cave	Location only
Light Thread	The Cave	Cliff
Mallet	The Cave	Ibis, Crater, Cliff, Avalanche, Temple, The Necklace
Key	The Cave	Location only
Shaver	The Cave	Location only
Crystal	Leaving Yuna	Location only
Palm leaf	Ibis	Location only
Oyster	Ibis	Location only
Pearl	Ibis	The Necklace
Scepters	Crater	Location only
Gourd	Crater	Location only
Gem	Crater	Location only
Conch	Prayer scrolls	Avalanche
Chain	Plateau	Location only
Shield	Plateau	Avalanche
Strap	The Train	Avalanche
Diamond	Statues Room	Room of Mirrors
Mirror	Room of Mirrors	Room of Pictures
Music Box	Room of Pictures	Location only

INHERIT THE EARTH: QUEST FOR THE ORB

BY
STACEY PORTNOY

TYPE
Animated Adventure

SYSTEM
IBM PC & CD-ROM (Required: 386 MHz+, 4 MB RAM, VGA, 1 MB hard disk.

Supports: Sound Blaster, Ad Lib & other major sound cards)

COMPANY
New World Computing

WITH A STORY SET IN A LAND POPULATED BY ANIMAL TRIBES RATHER THAN PEOPLE, INHERIT THE EARTH SOUNDS LIKE A GAME FOR KIDS. BUT THE FASCINATING STORY WILL PLEASE ADULTS TOO, MAKING IT EXCELLENT FAMILY ENTERTAINMENT. IT'S THE STORY OF A FOX NAMED RIF, WHOM THE OTHER ANIMALS HAVE BLAMED FOR STEALING THE ORB OF STORMS. WITHOUT ITS WEATHER-FORECASTING POWERS, THEY ARE AT THE MERCY OF MOTHER NATURE, SO RIF AND HIS GIRLFRIEND FOX, RHENE, SET OUT TO TRACK IT DOWN AND RETURN IT. EEAHH THE ELK AND OKK THE BOAR JOIN THE QUEST TO FIND THE ORB, WHICH IS EXEMPLIFIED BY A HIGHLY STYLISTIC CARTOON TREATMENT AND EXTENSIVE DIALOGUE THAT YOU GET TO HEAR

IN THE CD VERSION (OVER FOUR HOUR'S WORTH).

THE INTERFACE IS REMINISCENT OF LUCASARTS' FIRST GRAPHIC ADVENTURES, ENABLING YOU TO CREATE SENTENCES BY CLICKING ON VERBS FROM A LIST AND OBJECTS PICTURED BELOW. AFTER A LONG ANIMATED CARTOON THAT SETS UP THE TALE, THE QUEST TAKES YOU THROUGH NUMEROUS LANDSCAPES AND LOCATIONS WHOSE ARTISTIC QUALITY GIVES THE GAME THE FEELING OF A FEATURE-LENGTH ANIMATED CARTOON. THE EXTENSIVE DIALOGUE, PARTICULARLY IN THE CD VERSION, TRULY BRINGS THIS UNUSUAL WORLD TO LIFE. NEWCOMERS TO ADVENTURE WILL APPRECIATE THE FACT THAT THE ONLY THING HARD TO DO IN *INHERIT THE EARTH* IS GET STUCK FOR DAYS.

THE SOLUTION

PART I: THE UNKNOWN LANDS

MARKET FAIRE

Exit the tent and follow the path to the northwest.

Go northeast at the intersection.

Just past the "eat" sign is a tent.

Enter it and speak to the fortuneteller about all. She will tell you to search the scene of the crime and to find Elara.

Return to main road and follow it northwest until you come to an open tent on the right side of the road.

Enter tent and speak to the moneychanger.

Ask for advice and agree to sell the silver medallion for 15 credits.

Continue northwest on the main road until you reach the end and the overhead map.

SCENE OF THE CRIME

Go to the sanctuary.

Open temple gate, then temple door.

Follow path and go straight at the intersection.

Open the door that leads into the temple grounds.

Go into the Orb Temple and speak to Elara.

Return to the overhead map and walk to the forest in the upper-left corner.

Go left and talk to the King.

Ask King about Elara.

Return to Elara and give her the token, and she will open the sanctuary gates.

Return to the intersection and go northwest.

Enter the garden and turn left.

In the lower left hand corner of the second plot, get the bucket.

Leave the plot and go southeast until you reach a fountain.

Use bucket on the fountain.

Go to the upper northern corner, where there is a footprint.

Look at the footprint and pick up the berries next to it.

Go to the castle.

CASTLE

Talk to the boar sentry and choose the first option.

Walk around hallway until you enter the mud bath of the Boar King.

Go into the mud, talk to the King and see Rhene.

Leave the mud bath.

When you shake off the mud, you will discover a ring with a wolf's head crest on it.

SIST & THE FOOTPRINT

Go to the cave and talk to the doorkeeper about all.

Confuse him so you can get by to see the leader.

While Eeahh and Okk are creating a diversion, put on the rat cloak and enter the tunnels.

To find Sist in the northeast section of the tunnels: go northeast, southeast, northeast, southeast, northeast (through the library and past the chairs).

From the library, head northeast, southeast and northeast (into the sundial room, exiting through the right doorway).

From the sundial room, go southwest, southeast, southwest, northwest, northwest, and northeast to Sist.

Talk to Sist, who tells you he wants a cast of the print and tells you plaster can be obtained at the Ferret Village.

Go to the Ferret Village.

Go east and south to the path.

Go southeast, northeast, then southeast through the arch to the town square.

To the right is a building with a blue cobblestone step. Enter and talk to glassmaker.

Leave and walk towards the fence (left) and open the door to reach the Ferret Merchant.

Look at bags (of plaster) in front of merchant.

Talk to him and select "give him the money."

Return to the sanctuary garden where you found the footprint.

Use bag of plaster with bucket of water.

Use bucket of wet plaster with footprint.

Pick up the plaster cast.

Return to cave and distract (confuse) doorkeeper to enter tunnels and see Sist.

Give him the plaster cast and then give him the berries.

LENS

Go to house on map and enter Tycho's home.

Ask Tycho about all.

Offer to fix lightcatcher in exchange for map.

Go to the Ferret Village and see the glassmaker.

Give him the piece of broken glass and agree to meet at the lodge.

Go northwest, southwest, southeast, then northeast.

Open the door and talk to Sakka, who will help only if you pass the tanagram test.

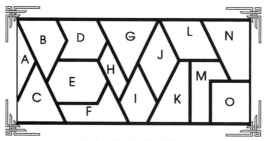

Lodge Initiation Test

A: Screwdriver   F: Wood plane   K: Shears
B: C-clamp   G: Mallet   L: Hatchet
C: Pliers   H: Level   M: Ruler
D: Wood clamp   I: Claw hammer   N: Saw
E: Twine   J: Tape measure O: Paint brush

AFTER PASSING THE TEST

Talk to the Orb of Hands.

The Orb is unfamiliar with the origin of the glass and the name lightcatcher, and will suggest that seek out the Rats.

Return to Sist and give him the broken glass.

Return to the lodge and talk to the Orb.

The Glassmaker will fix the lens, but it will still be too rough.

Ask Sakka for advice, then ask the Orb for advice to learn about red clay.

Okk will tell you it can be found in the Boar King's mudbath. Go there.

Bribe sentry and visit the Boar King.

When you leave, some mud will be in your inventory.

Back at the lodge, give the mud to the Glassmaker, who will now fix the lens.

Take the repaired lens to Tycho, who will give you a map.

When you leave, Elara's servant gives you a letter to deliver to her sister Alamma.

PART II: THE WILD LANDS

CASTLE DUNGEON

Go to the Dog Castle, which is northeast of Tycho's home.

At the entrance, say you will tell some jokes to the Prince.

After being locked up, pick up the wooden bowl and use it on the cell door to call a guard.

Ask the guard for food, then for a spoon.

Eat the food.

Use spoon on the loose stone block.

Remove loose block.

Exit through the tunnel.

Save the game.

IN THE MAZE

As you walk along the tunnel, you will fall into a maze. If the roaming dragon touches you, you will fall off, climb back up at a random spot and land next to the Prince. To get through the maze, follow these directions:

Go northwest (through an arch). Move northwest (over a bridge). Northeast.

Southeast. Northeast. Southeast. Northeast (over another bridge).

After crossing the second bridge, go southeast. Northeast. Northeast. Northwest.

Southwest. Northwest. West. Southwest. Northwest. West. Southwest. Northwest. Southwest. Go southeast. Northeast. Northeast. Northwest. Southwest. Northwest. West. Southwest. Northwest. Southwest. Northwest (over a plank).

After crossing the plank, go northeast. Southeast. Northeast. Northeast. Northwest (over the plank). Follow wall to the door.

CAT VILLAGE

Walk south to the overhead map.

On Tycho's map is a teepee northwest of the castle. As you walk toward it, you will pass through a storm.

Enter the Cat Village, where you learn that the Chieftess's daughter is very sick.

After a good night's rest, talk to Prrowa and offer to help Mirrhp.

ELARA'S LETTER

Look at Tycho's map and go to the house northwest of you.

Talk to the door.

Use Elara's letter with the peephole three times.

Alamma will tell you about a folk remedy and its ingredients: honey (she gives you a bowl to collect it), catnip, and needle and thread.

THE CURE

Leave the cottage and go northwest over a bridge.

Walk towards the point where the lake meets the stream, and you will find the catnip.

Go to the gray block in the northeast corner of the map.

On the overhead map you'll see a quarry in the mountains.

Outside the mine entrance, pick up the flint chip and rope.

Walk towards the lake east of Alamma's cottage.

Follow the eastern edge up and around until you see an oak tree on a small hill: this is the honey tree.

Animals make the best party members in Inherit the Earth.

Pick up the dry twigs and use them.

Use flint chip with spoon to start a fire.

Once the bees are gone, use the bowl with the beehive to collect honey.

On Tycho's map you will see trees, which are forest clearings.

There are also clearings north of where the map ends. (On the overhead map they are brown square patches.) A traveling merchant moves from one clearing to another.

When you find Kylas Honeyfoot, talk to him and tell him you want the needle and thread, and you will trade the ring for it.

Return to Alamma and show her the ingredients; she will now make the healing salve.

Return to Claw Village. The path to the tents is behind the wildcat sentry.

Go into Prrowa's tent and give the salve to Mirrhp.

In return for your help, sedatives have been placed in the food supply of the castle guards so you can rescue your friends.

RESCUE AT DOG CASTLE

Enter the castle and follow the hall to the throne room.

Exit through the hallway on the right.

Follow this hall to the Prince's bedroom.

To get the key from the Prince, you must avoid stepping on floorboards that squeak.

Walk southeast two rows: to your right you will see part of a board that is raised; it will

131

squeak.

Walk toward the dresser (on the same row) and around this board.

Walk along the edge of the carpet and get the key.

Leave, and retrace your steps to the throne room.

Go out the left doorway.

Wind through the halls to the southwest corner of the castle.

Open cell door with key.

Retrace your path to the entrance and leave the castle.

PASSAGE TO NORTHERN ISLAND

Go to the quarry and enter the mine.

Try to pick up three green "fragments" of rock crystal three times.

Search the forest clearing for the merchant.

Talk to him, and you will see that he now carries a wolf ring.

Tell him you want to buy the ring and offer the crystal.

Go toward the honey oak tree.

Enter the gorge just west of the trees in the mountains.

Walk to the other side of the chasm.

Eeah will jump over.

Use the rope to make a rope bridge and walk to Eeah.

Once on the other side, walk to the right to go back out to the wilderness.

Walk northwest to the dock.

Talk to the old wolf and give him the wolf ring for the price of your passage.

On the boat, ask wolf about all.

PART III: THE NORTHERN ISLAND

ARRIVAL

Leave the dock and go northwest to the waterfall.

Go to the waterfall and talk to Shiala.

Pick any dialogue choice, as she will only answer one question.

Go to the dam, where you will be captured by wolves.

In prison, talk to the raccoon Chota about all; Shiala will soon rescue you.

Open the cage door and exit into the wolf camp.

To the left, enter the doorway that is under a banner.

Pick up the trophy on the tree stump.

Leave the tent and walk south to the wilderness.

The wolf camp is in the northeast part of the island.

Go east and follow the coast around until you return to the dock.

Along the eastern edge and across from the mountains, note the seaside cliff you pass.

Kylas the merchant will be at the dock.

Tell him you want to buy the oil lamp; bargain with him.

ANCIENT RUINS

Go toward the dam and across the bridge to the ruins.

Open the sliding door on the second building to the left.

Enter and pick up the spool of cable on the ground.

Leave and go to the next building on the left.

You will only be able to open the door partly, as it is rusted.

Use oil lamp on door to loosen it, then open the door.

Inside, get screwdriver on work table.

DAM

Go to the dam.

Follow the path around and walk toward the hillside.

At the top of the hill is a white building.

Use screwdriver to open stuck door.

Look at the box with glowing numbers: you will see a door on the back.

Open the box, and a metallic cylinder appears in your inventory.

ADMIN 14

Go to the seaside cliff.

Below the cliff is a keycard in a nest.

Use the cable to get the keycard.

Go back to the ancient ruins.

Turn right just past the fence.

At the end of the building is a sign: Admin 14.

Open door and go in.

Use the keycard on the panel with the glowing lights, and the doorway opens up.

Follow the hall to the office.

Pick up the triangular device on the desk.

Leave the building.

WATERFALL

Go to the waterfall.

Go to the gap between the two falls, then to the waterfall to the left to get behind it.

Walk to the passage to reach Shiala's lair.

Talk to her.

Use the triangular device with the cylinder, then use it on the iron hatch to open it.

Go into the tunnel and toward the distant light.

Go to the end of the corridor.

Climb a ladder twice.

Go upstairs and up another ladder to reach the raccoon Chota.

Confront him.

ORBS & STUFF

Object	See this Section for Location	Also See Section(s)
Fortuneteller	Market Faire	Location only
Bucket	Scene of the Crime	Sist & the Footprint
Berries	Scene of the Crime	Sist & the Footprint
Wolf Ring	Castle	The Cure, Passage to Northern Island
Plaster	Sist & the Footprint	Location only
Lightcatcher	Lens	Location only
Spoon	Castle Dungeon	The Cure
Honey	The Cure	Elara's Letter
Catnip	The Cure	Elara's Letter
Needle	The Cure	Elara's Letter
Thread	The Cure	Elara's Letter
Flint Chip	The Cure	Location only
Rope	The Cure	Passage to Northern Island
Bowl	Castle Dungeon, Elara's Letter	The Cure
Cable	Ancient Ruins	Admin 14
Screwdriver	Ancient Ruins	Dam
Metallic Cylinder	Dam	Waterfall
Keycard	Admin 14	Location only
Triangular Device	Admin 14	Waterfall

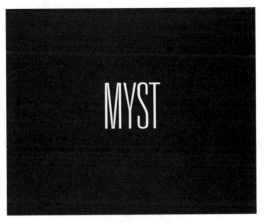

MYST

BY
FRED PHILIPP
& CLANCY SHAFFER

TYPE
Graphic Adventure

SYSTEM
Macintosh CD, IBM CD (Required: 386/16+, 2 MB XMS, VGA, CD drive, mouse. Supports: Sound Blaster, SVGA, VESA. Recommended: double-spin CD drive)

COMPANY
Broderbund

HE TITLE OF THIS GAME WAS INSPIRED BY JULES VERNE'S NOVEL, MYSTERIOUS ISLAND, FOR YOU START OUT STRANDED ON A DESERT ISLAND FILLED WITH ODD DEVICES AND BUILDINGS. THE GOAL IS TO ESCAPE, WHICH INVOLVES SOLVING THE PUZZLES LEFT BEHIND BY THE ISLAND'S FORMER INHABITANTS AND VISITING THE FOUR WORLDS MADE ACCESSIBLE BY THEM. MOST OF THE QUEST CENTERS ON BOOKS, FROM TRAVEL BOOKS TO CODE BOOKS TO THE CRUCIAL BLUE AND RED BOOKS. BY FINDING COLOR-CODED PAGES FOR THE LATTER, YOU UNCOVER MESSAGES AND CLUES THAT LEAD YOU FURTHER INTO THE HEART OF THE MYSTERY. GRAPHICALLY MYST IS A STUNNER, FEATURING PHOTOFANTASTIC 3-D ILLUSTRATIONS REINFORCED BY SYMPHONIC MUSIC AND STARTLING SOUND EFFECTS. YOU CAN TURN AROUND IN A LOCATION AND ZOOM IN ON THINGS, EXPERIENCING GRAPHIC EFFECTS THAT ADD EVEN MORE TO THE SENSE OF A "VIRTUAL ADVENTURE."

THE CAPTIVATING STORY AND ITS SLICK PRESENTATION MAKE MYST ONE OF THE BEST MULTI-MEDIA QUESTS YET.

THE SOLUTION

THE DOCK

Walk along the dock and turn on the Marker Switch.

NOTE FROM ATRUS

Go upstairs to the Giant Cog and pull the switch.

Go back and take the redwood steps leading up.

Pick up note lying on ground, read and drop it.

DIMENSIONAL IMAGER

Return to the dock, open door in wall, enter and walk down ramp to the Dimensional Imager.

Turn around and read note on wall for settings.

After turning dial to settings, press green button, turn around and press button on Imager for Image. (Settings are 40, 67, 47. Also set dial to 08 and note Image.)

PLANETARIUM

Return to where you found the note and continue up the hill to a door and a switch on your right.

Pull switch, open door and enter building (note the hi-tech dentist's chair).

Turn around and press button on wall: you're now in the Planetarium.

Turn on the lights and exit building.

Continue upstairs to the top.

ORIENTATION

Around a corner and ahead of you is a distant Rocket Ship; to your left, a path leads down between a forest of pine trees.

Enter the arch to your right, and you'll be in the Tower.

THE BOOKS

Examine the map of the island.

Check out the Red and Blue Books.

Pick up the Red and Blue Pages beside the books, put the pages in the same colored books and listen to the messages (the static is normal).

Listen carefully for bits of information: this is your first contact with the brothers Sirrus and Achenar, sons of Atrus and Catherine.

BOOKCASE

Move closer to the bookcase.

Pick up and read the larger, more defined, unburned books: there are four travel books and a code book.

Each travel book tells about a different Age invented by Atrus.

Closely examine the drawings in the books for partial clues on how to get to the different Ages; write down or draw clues.

You will also learn about Sirrus, Achenar, Atrus and Catherine.

SWITCHES

Exit the Tower, head to the Rocket Ship and pull the switch.

Return to the Tower, go down forest path to bird bath and pull switch.

Continue further along and turn on the switches right and left at the Power House and Boiler Room.

You have now turned on seven of the eight switches (the eighth one is by the Clock Tower, but you don't have enough clues to reach it now).

MYST ISLAND MAP

Return to the Tower and click on the painting of stairs to turn the bookcase into stairs with an opening behind them.

Click on map of the island and hold hand down on tower schematic to produce rotating beam.

The beam turns red at the Giant Cog, Sunken Ship, Boiler Room and Rocket Ship.

FINDING CLUES

At each of the red beam locations, repeat this process:

Stop beam when it's on a location and red.

Enter stairs behind bookcase and proceed down hallway to elevator, turn around and press "Library" button.

Exit and climb ladder with "Book" symbol on it and climb to top.

Look out slit window to see where the beam is pointing.

Climb down ladder and go around elevator to ladder with the "Key" symbol.

Climb ladder to top and go to plaque on the wall.

Write down clue(s) specific to that location.

Descend to elevator, then to Tower, and return to map of the island.

To return bookcase to normal so you can open the arch and exit the Tower, click on painting of the arch depicting the exterior of the Tower.

REACHING THE FOUR AGES

You may enter the Four Ages in any order. The following section first lists the clues for each Age, which you can use to figure out how to reach the Ages. If you prefer, skip to the "Action" section of each Age for specific instructions.

STONESHIP AGE

Clues: Beam points to the Sunken Ship, window shows the Planetarium.

Book shows constellations.

Three dates: OCT 11, 1984, 10:04 AM; JAN 17, 1207, 5:46 AM; NOV 23, 9791, 6:57 PM.

Actions: Go to planetarium, turn off lights, sit in chair and operate device.

Set device to each of the three dates and times.

Draw constellations.

Return to Tower and compare drawings with constellations in book on Stoneship Age: this will show the Spider, Snake and Leaf.

Go to the eight standards near the bird bath with the model ship inside.

Change the Spider, Snake and Leaf symbols to green, all the others to red.

The ship at the dock will surface.

Myst is remarkable for its fine graphics.

MECHANICAL AGE

Clues: Beam points to Giant Cog.

Window shows Clock Tower: numbers 2:40 and 2, 2, 1.

Actions: Take path to Clock Tower.

Turn wheels on ground until clock reads 2:40 (right wheel moves minute hand, left wheel moves hour hand).

A path of gears will appear, leading to clock.

Cross gears and pull marker switch #8.

Enter Tower.

Set gears inside to 2, 2, 1.

Pull down and hold left handle to rotate lower dial to 1.

Rotate center dial and stop at 3.

This should now show 3, 3, 1.

Pull down and release right handle twice.

This will set dial to 2, 2, 1, and the Giant Cog near the dock will open.

CHANNELWOOD AGE

Clues: Beam points to Boiler Room.

Window shows Tall Tree.

Numbers 7, 2, 4.

Actions: Go to Boiler Room northeast of the Clock Tower.

Go around back and note Tall Tree.

Return to Boiler room and enter.

Turn around and open safe on wall with combination 7, 2, 4. Get match and light it by striking it on matchbox in the safe.

Turn around and turn wheel clockwise all the way on.

You will hear the noise of the Tall Tree rising.

Turn the wheel counter-clockwise all the way, until the flame in the boiler goes out.

Exit building, go to Tall Tree (Watch Tower) and wait until opening in tree (elevator) appears.

Enter elevator to go down to Travel Book.

SELENITIC AGE

Clues: Beam points to Rocket Ship.

Window shows Power House.

Number 59.

Book shows picture of a keyboard, numbered 5, 1, 4, 2, 3.

Actions: Go to Power House off path near bird bath.

Set line voltage to 59 by hitting buttons 1, 4, 7, 8, 10.

Go to Rocket Ship and enter: on right is an Organ, on left a set of slider switches.

Listen to the notes on the keyboard, then set the sliders to the exact notes in the order 1, 2, 3, 4, 5.

Pull the lever to make the Travel Book appear.

Another way to solve this puzzle: count the keys on the organ, from the left, and set the sliders that way. This way you would set the sliders at 8, 20, 23, 13, 6.

SOLVING THE FOUR AGES

After completing the previous section for each of the Ages, you can enter each of them and solve them in any order you choose.

STONESHIP AGE

Go to the recently surfaced ship.

Go downstairs to Travel Book and click on book.

ORIENTATION

To your left is an umbrella with pump switches #1, 2, 3 (from left to right).

Ahead is Tunnel #1, behind you a ship.

To your right is lighthouse; right and up the stairs is Tunnel #2.

Past the tunnel and up the hill is a telescope.

LIGHTHOUSE

Hit pump switch #3 to drain the lighthouse.

Go to lighthouse.

Click on key on floor.

Go downstairs to chest.

Open spigot to drain chest, then close spigot.

Hit pump switch #3 to flood lighthouse, then go to lighthouse.

GENERATOR

Click on key, unlock chest and get key from inside chest.

Climb ladder to trapdoor and unlock it with key.

Enter room.

Rotate handle on generator until batteries are charged.

TELESCOPE

Go up hill to telescope and rotate until you see the lighthouse with a flashing beam of light.

Note degrees of rotation (135).

Return to pump switches.

TUNNEL #2

Hit switch #2 to drain tunnels.

Go to Tunnel #2: the lights are now on.

Follow tunnel to door into Achenar's bedroom.

Turn around and go back up stairs to the next landing.

Look for a small square red mark on the lower left wall.

Click on it to open the secret door.

COMPASS ROOM

Enter chamber and go to large compass on floor.

Set compass to 135 degrees (push 12th button, clockwise from North [0 degrees] at tip of lower right red triangle).

This is the switch to turn on the lights in the ship.

BLUE PAGE

Exit to tunnel and go to bedroom.

Examine map file cabinet to read half of note.

Check out disk with holograms of rose and skull.

Look at bed and get Blue Page.

Note: If the lights go out, get those generator batteries powered up again.

THE SHIP

Hit pump switch #1 to drain ship.

Go to ship, descend to the door, open it and enter.

Descend, then go left and right to a table.

Click on table to produce a book.

Click on book to return to Myst Island.

BLUE BOOK

Put Blue Page in Blue Book and listen to message.

Note: You will have to visit each Age twice to retrieve both pages.

RED PAGE

Return to Stoneship Age and drain tunnels again.

Go to Tunnel #1, descend to door and enter Sirrus' bedroom.

To get Red Page, examine table with drawer, then the dresser.

RED BOOK

Drain the ship, descend to the Red Book and return to Myst.

Insert Red Page in Red Book and listen to message.

MECHANICAL AGE

Go to giant gear at end of dock, which is now open.

Enter gear, descend and click on book.

FORTRESS

To your left, note device with four buttons.

Straight ahead is a short, dead end extension: take path to the right, leading to the Fortress, and enter.

SIMULATOR

Take the right fork and follow hall to Achenar's bedroom.

Examine the Fortress Rotation Simulator, which is a hologram to practice on for the real Fortress Rotator you will soon find.

(Note that proper rotation of the Fortress will allow you access to four previously inaccessible islands surrounding the Fortress.)

BLUE PAGE

To enter the hidden room, click on the panel on the wall; it's near the floor and left of throne chair.

Note mask and cage. Then click on cage.

Pick up Blue Page.

BASEMENT

Exit bedroom through other door and along hall to open door with red button and elevator in front of you.

Pressing button opens floor, exposing stairs down.

Go down and over to rotational device.

Rotate device until red symbol appears.

Exit room and press button to close stairs.

ELEVATOR

Enter elevator.

Press up button, then middle button.

Wait for six beeps, then exit.

FORTRESS ROTATION CONTROL

Rotate controls until you hear a distinctive sound: chirps, beeps, whoosh, ping.

Stop control at each sound, then exit Fortress.

The Fortress rotates, allowing access to four islands surrounding it.

ISLANDS

Two islands, north and east, have podiums with symbols.

Visit all four islands and write down the symbols.

Rotate Fortress back to its original position.

SYMBOL'S DEVICE

Exit Fortress and return to where you arrived at the symbols device.

Enter symbols in the order shown in the accompanying illustration.

Press button to open staircase.

Go down and click on the book to return to Myst.

Listen to Blue Page, then return to Mechanical Age for Red Page.

SIRRUS' BEDROOM

Enter Fortress and follow the left hall to Sirrus' bedroom.

Examine the room, then click below the southwest corner of the wall hanging to open the hidden room.

Enter hidden room, pick up the note on the wine rack and read it.

Open chest and get Red Page.

Return to Myst and listen to Red Page message.

CHANNELWOOD AGE

Use Tall Tree elevator to travel to Channelwood Age.

Listen to those frogs!

WINDMILL

Go left to end, then right for awhile to a windmill on top of a hill.

Note valves connecting pipes along waterway.

Inside windmill, open spigot at base of water tower.

Hit control switch on left to empty water into waterway pipes.

CAGE WITH TREE HOUSE

Open valves along waterway to divert water to cage with tree house above.

Enter elevator cage, close door, pull switch to ascend.

LEVEL 2

Go forward to second tree house, right to second tree house, then right to the next tree house.

Locate switch in tree house and turn it on, unlocking door at base of the spiral staircase.

LEVEL 3

Descend staircase and open door.

Go to first valve in front of you and divert water to elevator above staircase.

Climb staircase, enter elevator, close door and hit switch to reach level 3.

BLUE PAGE

From the elevator, the Blue Page is in a bedroom straight ahead and to your right.

Check out the holographic device while you're there.

When returning to the elevator, go straight ahead and examine the Masks Room.

RED PAGE

From the elevator, go left into the hut.

Look in dresser drawer for Red Page.

Look under bed for second half of note regarding Vault Access.

REPAIRING BRIDGE

Grab either page and head back down to the waterways.

Locate the device at the apparent dead end of the pipe, to the east and around a tree.

Go back and divert water to device.

Pull switch on device to make a bridge appear.

ANOTHER ELEVATOR

Cross bridge and proceed to third elevator.

Turn around, look to your left and turn on the switch, which connects a new set of pipes to the elevator.

Return and divert water through the new set of pipes.

GETTING OUT

Cross bridge and return to the elevator, which now works.

Enter, close door, and go up.

Exit and go to the Travel Book.

Travel back to Myst and listen to the message.

GOING BACK

Return to the Channelwood Age.

Divert water at staircase valve only.

Get the next page, go to the elevator, and use book to return to Myst.

Listen to second page.

SELENITIC AGE

Exit ship.

Descend ramp to road to structure with sealed portal door (underground caverns).

Note lock with five sounds code and slider bars.

FIRE

Continue down road to stairs left of road going up.

Climb stairs to tower with antenna.

Press red button on podium to activate fire icon.

Look down chasm and note microphone on cable.

WATER

Descend stairs and take path to right.

Climb stairs and go between trees.

Follow path to Oasis.

Note well to right, and microphone.

Push button on podium to activate water icon.

Pick up Blue Page on podium.

CLOCK

Return to main path, then go left.

Go past stairs to the chasm, then go right to Clock Tower.

Push button.

CRYSTAL MUSIC

Follow path along peninsula to Y-branch.

Go right to stairs leading to the Crystal Columns.

Follow brick passage to platform.

Note Red Page on podium for later reference.

Push button.

WIND

Return to Y-branch, then go right along the peninsula to podium at the pier.

Push button and climb down ladder.

Pull switch to turn on lights in tunnel.

Go through tunnel to next ladder, then up.

You will emerge on an island in the lagoon.

Follow stairs up to podium.

Open doors on podium to expose a Control Panel.

CONTROL PANEL

Sequence

Select location icon.

Rotate camera to that location.

Press large button.

Repeat for all five locations.

Settings

Rotate camera to the following settings: 15, 153.4, 212.2, 130.3, 55.6. This will align the sounds code that activates the Portal door.

PORTAL

Return to Portal door and enter the five sounds sequence:

1. Music
2. Water
3. Wind
4. Fire
5. Ticking

Push button to open door.

SUBWAY

Follow metallic passageway to the chamber with the pod-like car.

Push the blue button, enter and sit in chair.

Push the forward control.

Note compass heading.

Go: north, west, north, east, east, south, south, west, southwest, west, northwest, northeast, north, and southeast.

Push blue button and exit.

Exit mazerunner and follow corridor to chamber.

Click on Travel Book to return to Myst.

ENDGAME

Listen to either brother's final message.

Check pattern on page 158 in the code book in the bookcase (middle shelf, right side).

VAULT ACCESS

Go to Marker Switch at the dock and turn it off.

Get white page from vault.

Return to Tower.

FIREPLACE

Enter fireplace.

Click on upper left button.

Enter pattern on slate that appears.

Click on button again, which rotates the fireplace and provides access to a Secret Chamber.

SECRET CHAMBER

Exit elevator and go forward.

Defy the brothers' request by clicking on Green Book.

Click on picture of Atrus and listen to message.

Click the White Page on Atrus to travel to Dunny.

DUNNY

Give White Page to Atrus when he asks for it.

Atrus will vanish.

Wait for Atrus to return.

Click on Linking Book on desk to return to Myst.

Note that the Red and Blue Books have been burned in your absence.

ORBS & STUFF

Object	See this Section for Location	Also See Section(s)
Giant Cog	Note from Atrus	Myst Island Map, Mechanical Age
Red Book	The Books	Red Book, Dunny
Blue Book	The Books	Blue Book, Dunny
Red page	The Books, Red Page, Symbol's Device, Sirrus' Bedroom, Crystal Music	Red Book
Blue Page	The Books, Blue Page, Water	Blue Book, Symbol's Device
Travel Books	Bookcase	"returns you to Myst Island"
Code Book	Bookcase	Endgame
Spigot	Lighthouse	Windmill
Pump switch #1	Orientation	The Ship
Pump switch #2	Orientation	Location only
Pump switch #3	Orientation	Lighthouse

THE PSYCHOTRON

BY
PAUL SHAFFER

TYPE
*Animated
Adventure*

SYSTEM
*IBM CD
(Required:
486SX/25+,
Windows 3.1,
4 MB RAM,
hard disk,
SVGA, dou-
ble-speed CD-
ROM drive,
MPC Level 2)*

COMPANY
*Merit
Software*

ABLE TO CONTROL SMALL MINDS WITH A SINGLE TOP SECRET DEVICE? THAT'S THE PSYCHOTRON, THE HIGH-TECH RESULT OF RUSSIAN RESEARCH INTO PARANORMAL PHENOMENAE. AFTER THE CIA MANAGES TO BUY IT FROM A CORRUPT RUSSIAN SCIENTIST, THE DEVICE WINDS UP A ON PLANE THAT CRASHES IN THE HILL OF VIRGINIA. THE PSYCHOTRON TURNS UP MISSING, THE CREW TURNS UP DEAD, AND YOU TURN UP TO SOLVE THE MYSTERY. AS A CIA AGENT, YOU MUST FIND AND RECOVER THE MIND-CONTROL DEVICE BY EXPLORING VARIOUS LOCATIONS AND CONVERSING WITH OTHER AGENTS AND WITNESSES BY CHOOSING FROM SEVERAL DIALOGUE OPTIONS THAT CHANGE AS THE CONVERSATION PROGRESSES. YOU SPEND MORE TIME TALKING THAN EXPLORING, AND THESE SCENES ARE PRESENTED IN VIDEO FOR WINDOWS FILMS IN WHICH THE CHARACTERS ARE FULL DIGITIZED. AN UNUSUAL FEATURE ALLOWS TWO PEOPLE TO PLAY AT THE SAME TIME: AFTER ONE

COMPLETES A SECTION OF THE GAME, THE OTHER PLAYER CAN TRY TO GET A HIGHER SCORE IN THE SAME SECTION. THERE ARE NO OBJECTS TO PICK UP AND FIGURE OUT, WHICH DETRACTS FROM THE REALISM, BUT THE GOOD ACTING AND WELL-COMPOSED VIDEOS RESTORE THE "YOU ARE THERE" SENSATION. A LIGHTWEIGHT QUEST FOR EXPERIENCED ADVENTURERS, THE PSYCHOTRON STILL OFFERS A CHALLENGE FOR NOVICES — AND ANYONE WHO ENJOYS A GOOD SPY MOVIE.

THE SOLUTION

CIA OFFICES

Examine CIA offices.

Examine Polenski's office.

Examine document in cabinet, message on computer monitor and tape player (activate tape).

Examine Chang's office.

Examine message on computer, tape recorder in bookcase (activate tape), and TV.

Examine Gonzalez' office.

Examine message on computer monitor, phone (press playback for message), and memo in cabinet.

THE SAFE

Examine Knight's office.

Examine lamp (noting safe code: translate using letter clusters as numbers on phone).

Examine tape recorder (activate tape, noting recorder code).

Examine painting (safe).

Enter safe code: 7425 (write down security access codes for later). Exit offices.

MEMORIAL SERVICE

Go to memorial services.

Talk to gravedigger.

Answer him with these responses: 2, 2, 1, 2, 1.

Talk to Stone.

Answer him with these responses: 1, 2, 2.

Talk to Amber.

Answer him with these responses: 1, 2, 2.

Talk to Rivers.

Answer him with these responses: 2, 2, 1.

You are transported to the Crash Site.

You must play the card game in Psychotron four times to complete this part of the game.

········

CRASH SITE

Use these responses: 2, 2, 1, 2.

Push left lever on recorder.

Enter recorder code: 3333.

Push right lever (message plays).

Enter barn.

Examine first aid kit, parachutes and canisters under seat.

Enter rear of house.

Use these responses: 1, 2, 1, 2.

CARD GAME

Join game.

Ante up and bet a large amount.

Bet a lot.

Bet a lot and ask about Steve.

Answer: 1.

Bet reasonably.

See, raise and call.

Join game for second hand.

Match current bet.

Stay in.

Stay in and ask about Steve.

Say "You beat me, Jimmy" and fold.

Answer: 2.

Join game for third hand.

Bet a lot.

Bet a lot again.

"So, Phil, where did you pick Steve up?"

Bet reasonably.

Call Phil's bluff.

Answer: 1

Join game for last hand.

Stay in.

Deny any cheating, then leave the table.

COMPOUND

Examine foyer.

Examine parachute and phone.

Go to communications center.

Examine phone, body and TV monitors (examining two different active monitors).

Go to lab.

Examine generator, body and file in cabinet (note code instructions).

With Psychotron, enter security access codes in their proper order.

Enter the five-digit code first (81568), the three-digit code next, then the six-digit code (828970), and finally, the four-digit code (2217).

Return to lab.

BACK AT THE LAB

Examine generator and body again.

Enter foyer.

Examine phone and parachute again.

Go to communications center.

Examine body and phone again.

Your boss appears and asks you a couple questions to justify your investigation. Answer:

1. Richard Marx
2. Under psychic influence
3. To enhance Russian uprising
4. Plane made an unscheduled stop
5. To end influence on Russian Communists
6. Act like a hero for saving Russia

ENDGAME

Turn Psychotron on Nardini boys.

RAVENLOFT: STRAHD'S POSSESSION

BY
**CLANCY SHAFFER &
FRED PHILLIP**

TYPE
Fantasy Role-playing

SYSTEM
IBM (Required: 386+, 4MB RAM, VGA, DOS 5+, hard disk. Recommended: 486DX 33+ fast video card, 300 KB data transfer, 320ms access time & MSCDEX 2.1+ for CD version. DOS printer required to print maps. Supports: major sound cards (100% compatible Sound Blaster required for speech)

COMPANY
SSI/Electronic Arts

AVENLOFT, WORLD OF THE UNDEAD, IS THE BACKDROP FOR AN INTENSE ROLE-PLAYING ODYSSEY. A MULTIPLE-CHARACTER RPG, IT RESEMBLES BUT SURPASSES SSI'S GOLD BOX SERIES IN PRODUCTION VALUES AS WELL AS STORY AND GAMEPLAY. YOUR GOAL IS TO COLLECT A NUMBER OF ITEMS NECESSARY FOR OPENING A MAGICAL GATE AND ESCAPE RAVENLOFT — IF YOU LIVE LONG ENOUGH TO REACH RAVENLOFT CASTLE AND DEFEAT ITS VAMPIRE RULER, COUNT STRAHD VON ZAROVICH.

NATURALLY COMBAT CONSTITUTES A MAJOR PORTION OF GAMEPLAY. MOST OF THE PUZZLES, IN FACT, CONSIST OF EXAMINING WALLS FOR SECRET DOORS AND PORTALS. MAZES, TRAP DOORS, SPINNERS — ALL THE MOST MADDENING ASPECTS OF A CLASSIC DUNGEON CRAWL ARE IN STORE FOR THE INTREPID ADVENTURER WHO SEEKS FUN AND GAMES IN THIS TWISTED LAND. WHILE THE GRAPH-

ICS AND SOUNDS, AS WELL AS THE STORY, ARE FIRST-RATE, THEY ARE EVEN BETTER IN THE CD VERSION. THE CD FEATURES FULL-VOICE SUPPORT FOR MONSTERS AND THE NPCS YOU MAY BUMP INTO (BUT NOT FOR YOUR PARTY MEMBERS), EXTRA CINEMATIC SCENES AND MORE. STILL, *RAVENLOFT'S* INTENSE FOCUS ON COMBAT, WHICH ODDLY LACKS AN AUTO-COMBAT OPTION, AND LACK OF THE SORT OF PUZZLES FOUND IN *LANDS OF LORE* AND OTHER CONTEMPORARY RPGS, MAKE IT BEST-SUITED FOR HARD-CORE ORC-SLAYERS.

THE SOLUTION

GENERAL

Closely scrutinize all interior locations for buttons, levers and illusionary walls. Check your Automap often to find hidden rooms or areas. Pick up, read and keep all books, for some will be necessary to complete the quest. Continually upgrade your armor, weapons and magic as you progress.

STARTING OUT

After you create or select your first two characters, the quest begins in the Forgotten Realms Forest. A good combination is a Fighter and a Cleric/Mage. Note: a character cannot cast a Mage Spell while wearing armor. From the outset, go south to the Assassin, kill him, and pick up all items he drops. You will be teleported to the Woods.

WOODS

Go west to the abandoned hut.

Check out the skeleton.

Look for a button on the south wall and open the trapdoor.

Go down to the hidden underground chamber.

Open two doors using buttons on walls.

Enter rooms and gather up weapons, armor, scrolls and potions.

Exit the hut.

Go to the southeast corner of the woods and rescue Fhalken.

Have him join your party and pick up all the loot scattered around.

Head back toward the hut, then go west to exit the woods to Old Svalich Road South.

OLD SVALICH ROAD SOUTH

Go north and talk to the Gypsy. (You will meet him again near the end of the quest.) Continue north until you reach Barovia.

BAROVIA

BURGOMASTER

Head northwest to the large walled enclosure with an opening on the east side.

Enter and continue west to enter the Burgomaster's Mansion.

Check all rooms for scrolls, books and the like.

Go to the room in the southeast corner and talk to the Burgomaster.

STRAHD

Accept Strahd's invitation to travel to the Castle.

Inside, enter the only unguarded door to the dining room.

Strahd will welcome you, give you a key to cavern west of Barovia, and transport you back to Barovia, where you arrive in the northwest corner.

CAVERN

IRMAGOG

Exit town via the northwest corner and go due west to the cavern door.

You'll meet Irmagog outside the door: have her join your party.

Enter door and use key on symbol on wall to open gateway.

VLADISLAV

Move slowly west, sideways and at an angle, to avoid the spinner.

Vladislav will insist upon joining you party. He's useless, but let him join just to get him out of your way.

GATEWAYS

Go west past the Lightning Bolts, then north to the gateway on the right.

Turn around and look south for a lever to open the gateway.

Enter and get Jade Cavern Key #1.

Return to the Lightening Bolts, go north to the corridor and east to the passageway.

Head north and pull the lever to open a gateway to the south.

Enter, open the next gateway and go to corner of the room to be teleported.

KEYS

Go west, then southwest to the next gateway and unlock it with Jade Key #1.

To kill Bone Golems, cast Turn Undead, then hack them to pieces.

Go south, then east to get Jade Key #2.

Backtrack to just short of where you arrived and go north to the niche to be teleported.

MORE KEYS

Go southwest to the next gateway and unlock it with Jade Key #2.

Enter the room and get Jade Key #3.

Go north to the niche and teleport.

Open the gateway in front of you with Jade Key #3.

Enter room, get Jade Key #4, go to the niche in the room and teleport again.

CHURCH VESTIBULE KEY

Open the gateway in front of you with Jade Key #4.

Go west to the next gateway and unlock it.

Enter, then go north to get the Church Vestibule key.

Head west to the gateway, which Irmagog will open.

Go west to the circular room, then through an illusionary wall to the west.

Don't step far into this room (watch out for a spinner).

Cast Dispel Magic to continue on into next circular room and go north and enter the Portal.

You will emerge back in the woods west of Barovia.

Irmagog and Vladislav will leave you.

Return to Barovia and take the northeast exit, then go north to the Old Church.

OLD CHURCH

MAIN FLOOR

Inside, use the Church Vestibule Key on right hole and enter.

Note the talking mirror and priest in a trance.

Go east and look for buttons on the wall to open up the next two rooms.

Get the Gold Church Key.

Go past the mirror west and north to the stairs down.

Pick up the Tome of Evil Artifacts lying on the ground.

Descend steps.

(While in the Church, be sure to collect these items for later use: Special Scrolls of Atonement, Cure Disease and Remove Curse.)

LOWER LEVEL

Check all rooms for loot and four pieces of parchment (your goal here).

Pull all levers and push all buttons.

Use the Gold Church Key to open locked doors.

Check your map often for items as you seek out the parchment.

PILLARS

In the room to the north you will see four large pillars.

A lever on the north side of the southeast pillar opens two doors in the room to west.

In the same room's northwest corner is an illusionary wall.

Go through the illusionary wall and head northeast to another such wall.

Then move north and west to a locked door (you'll open this one much later).

MORE SUBTLETIES

In a large room east of the locked door is lever that opens a door in the southwest corner of the room to your south.

In the southeast corner of the room to the south is a button that opens two doors on the west side of the room.

Exit west out of the large room into the Main Hall.

Go to the second room on the left (south), where you see a lantern hanging.

Go south, then northwest to an illusionary wall in the northwest corner.

Then go south through another illusionary wall, south to a door and enter it.

Face south and push the second button on the wall.

Go west and north to the next room.

Return to the door before you pushed the buttons, go to the northwest corner, through the illusionary wall and then head north.

Note the pile of Gold Bones in corner (don't get them now).

When you've recovered all four parchment pieces, return to the Main Floor.

MAIN FLOOR AGAIN

Put the four parchment pieces into the Tome of Evil Artifacts.

Hold Tome.

Go to mirror and use Tome.

The mirror will crack, freeing the priest.

Go and talk to priest, who will give you the Cemetery Key.

CEMETERY

FIRST VISIT TO CEMETERY

Exit the church and head to the Cemetery gates in the northeast corner.

Unlock them with the Cemetery Key and enter. (Note the locked vault to north.)

Go to the northeast corner and search for a Bag of Gold Dust.

A thief, Vuko, is to the south and will join the party if you choose.

BAROVIA (JEWELER'S GHOST)

Return to Barovia.

In the northeast area is a large building shaped like the number 3.

Enter and talk to the Ghost, who will give you a Bone Vault Key.

Your fighter will become possessed.

SECOND VISIT TO CEMETERY

Return to the cemetery and unlock the locked door with the Bone Vault Key.

Enter and kill the Lord of the Ghouls (Grymig).

Pick up the Bag of Gold Dust and the Rod of Rebirth.

Exit vault.

The Jeweler's Ghost appears, exorcises your fighter and gives you a Jeweler's Key.

**Guitarist from famous heavy metal band
does cameo in Ravenloft?**

BANSHEE

Head to the southeast corner, where a vault is inhabited by an invulnerable Banshee.

Outside the vault are two statues of sisters.

Hold and use the Gold Dust on each statue to eliminate Banshee.

Enter vault and descend to the Elven Warrior's Crypt.

167

ELVEN WARRIOR'S CRYPT

LOWER LEVEL ONE

Go east and talk to the Elf Spirit.

He will send you on quest to locate an Elven Signet that is hidden below.

Exit this room to the north and follow the corridor clockwise until you end up in the southeast corner with four closed doors.

TELEPORTERS & PYRE ELEMENTALS

Go west past the doors, then south and west to a niche.

Push button on the south wall.

Return to the four doors.

One door will now be open.

Enter the door, and you'll be teleported to the southwest section.

To slay the Pyre Elementals, use Magic Missiles.

Go west through the door and north to a button.

Push button.

Go south, then back east through two doors.

Head south and west, then teleport out.

FOUR DOORS

Return to the four doors and enter the newly opened door.

This takes you to the central section.

Go south all the way, then west to a button.

Push the button.

Go north all the way, then west and south to teleport out.

Enter next door to reach the southeast section.

Go east, south and west to a room.

Get key on floor.

Go south, west and north to exit.

Unlock the door near the niche button to descend.

LOWER LEVEL TWO

Search the entire level for seven buttons that are not associated with opening doors.

A niche in the southwest corner will teleport you to the southeast room.

There are many illusionary walls with daggers on them.

Search all illusionary walls until you find the Elven Tomb Key.

Return to where you entered and go north to the Elven Tomb.

Unlock it with the Elven Tomb Key and get the Elven Signet.

ELVEN CROWN

Return to the Spirit on illusionary walls upper level and give him the Elven Signet.

He will vanish, leaving Elven armor, weapon and Crown: take all.

Exit and return to Church.

CASTLE RAVENLOFT

RESURRECTION

Descend to the lower level of the church.

Go to the main corridor and enter the room on the right side, where you will find Gold Bones in the corner.

Use the Rod of Rebirth on them.

A Cleric will be resurrected and will give you the Sharp Iron Svalich Road Key.

CASTLE

Return to Barovia and take the north exit out to Svalich Road North.

Go north to gate of Castle.

Use Sharp Iron Svalich Road Key to unlock and enter.

CASTLE LEVELS

From the Main Floor, you can go down to the Larders of Ill Omen, up to the Court of the Count, up to Rooms of Weeping, and up to the Tower.

Search all areas.

You must locate a Tower Key and a Blood Bat key (both can be found by going up from the Larders of Ill Omen).

You will also need to locate a Silver Tower Key, so keep your eyes open.

DIRECT ROUTE

On the Main Floor, go to the large southeast room with stairs going up on its west side.

Go up to the Court, then up the next set of stairs to the Weeping Rooms.

Go to northeast corner and take stairs up to Tower.

TELEPORTING

Go north to door and unlock it with the Tower key.

Head northeast to the stairs up.

Teleport.

Go southeast, then north and teleport.

Go down the stairs to return.

In the northwest corner is a button.

Go south to the next button, which opens a door to the north.

Go north and east, then upstairs.

Teleport.

Go north to the door and unlock it with the Silver Tower key.

Enter and free Prisoner.

WERERAVEN FEATHER

Talk to the Prisoner.

He will tell you to seek Bray Martikova, tell you some passwords to use and give you a Wereraven Feather.

TAROKKA CARD

Return to Rooms of Weeping.

In the central, large room on north wall is an illusionary wall.

Enter the illusionary wall and go to the keyhole.

Unlock it with the Blood Bat Key, which opens the wall to the west.

Enter and get the Tarokka Card.

(Note stairs leading down: they go to the Dungeon. Strahd is down there, but you're not ready for him yet.)

Exit Castle and return to Barovia.

WEREWOLF CAVE QUEST

This is a side quest that will net you a Blood Key, which will open a red lock in a building in Barovia that yields various weapons, armor and potions. None of these are necessary to complete the game.

WEREWOLF CAVE

Go west out of Barovia to the cliffs, then north to enter the Werewolf Cave.

Move north and talk to the Werewolf.

ALBINO WOLF

Exit cave and go south to the area near the stone circle.

Wander around here until the Albino Wolf shows up.

Kill him and return to the werewolf.

Use the Special Scrolls of Atonement, Cure Disease and Remove Curse on the werewolf to set him free.

Return to Barovia.

RED GEM

Return to the cemetery building where you met the Jeweler's Ghost.

Go north to the locked door on the west wall.

Unlock it with the Jeweler's Key.

Enter and pick up the Red Gem.

Exit building.

RAVEN LORD

BLOOD ON THE VINE TAVERN

Locate Blood on the Vine tavern, a large building in the south-central area.

Enter and talk to the Gypsy and the Innkeeper.

The Gypsy wants fifteen Barovian coins for a Potion to neutralize the Poisonous Fog that you have encountered by now.

The innkeeper will direct you to the Merchant's Pride (if you have the Wereraven Feather).

Exit.

MERCHANT'S PRIDE

Go to the last building in the southeast corner and enter.

Then head north and talk to the human.

Drink Anodyne Potion.

Ravenlord appears and tells you about the Holy Symbol of Ravenkind, Sasha, a Cleric, and the three encrypted parchments.

MORE KEYS

The Raven Lord will give you a Ruby Catacomb Key and a Forgotten Gold Church Key.

He then tells you the location of the parchments (Church).

Next he gives you Sasha's Reading Glass and tells you how to use it.

You are now teleported to the Catacombs.

THE CATACOMBS

COINS

With the Ruby Key, you arrive in the southwest corner.

Your goal here is to find fifteen Barovian coins and a way out.

You must also locate three more Jewelled Keys.

Use the Ruby Key to unlock doors to the north and east.

SAPPHIRE KEY

From the southwest corner, head north to the second passage that goes east.

Go to the end room and get the Sapphire Key.

Return to the starting point.

Go east and search all rooms for coins.

Continue east, then north to the locked door and unlock it with the Sapphire key.

EMERALD KEY

Go north, west, north, west, north, east and south to the end room.

In the northwest corner is a button.

Push it to open the door, then advance and get the Emerald Key.

Return to the large room you first entered after opening the Sapphire lock.

On the east wall is a door for the Emerald key.

ONYX KEY

Go east, then due south to a wall with two buttons.

Push both to open areas to the north and south.

Continue to search all rooms for coins. You must find fifteen coins.

Go north, east and then south from the two buttons.

In the niche in the southwest corner of room is an illusionary wall. Enter it.

To your east is another niche with a button that opens a wall to the west.

Go west through it, then south to a niche in the southeast corner of the room and get the Onyx Key.

GETTING OUT

Return to the large room where you used the Emerald Key.

On the north wall is a button to open door to north.

Follow passage to Onyx lock.

Check the area to the southeast for coins, then unlock the door with the Onyx Key.

Go west along the path of fireballs, then south to a door with a button to the east.

Open door and explore for coins.

By now you must have fifteen coins; if not, reexplore all rooms until you have them.

Check your automap to make sure you covered all accessible areas.

LADDER UP

Return to the previous button.

Near a barrel on the west wall is another button.

Pushing it will open a trapdoor above a ladder on the wall next to the opening on the east wall (the one that is shooting the Fireballs in the Fireballs Corridor you just recently passed through in the northeast corner).

TRAPDOOR

Return to the Fireballs Corridor and head east to the wall with the Fireball opening.

Take the ladder up, go through the trapdoor and into the building in Barovia. (Check the automap for location.)

Exit and head back to the Church Door.

LOCKED CHURCH DOOR

TO LOWER LEVEL TWO

Return to Lower Level One of the Old Church.

Go to the hidden door with the lock (north of the Main Corridor you previously located).

Unlock this door with the Forgotten Gold Church Key and enter Lower Level 2.

PAGES

Your quest here is to locate three pages from Sasha's Lost Manuscript.

Go south and pick up the first page.

Go south, east and then south to an illusionary wall on the south wall.

Head east and north to get the Teardrop Church Key.

Return to where you found the first page.

READING GLASS

Pages two and three are in the northwest corner (behind illusionary wall) and in the northeast corner.

Examine all three pages with the Reading Glass (hold page in one hand, glass in the other, then click on page) to learn what you have to do next.

But first, go back to the Vine Tavern.

BLOOD ON THE VINE TAVERN

POTION

Give all fifteen coins to the Gypsy and get the Fog Potion, which enables you to get through the Poisonous Fog.

All fog areas are identical, so just pick any fog wall and go to it.

Use the Potion and enter the fog.

You will now be in the Undead Forest.

THE UNDEAD FOREST

SEEDS

Your initial objective is to find and pick up the four Seeds of Morninglory.

Bring up your map.

The first seed is within the Circle of Stones.

The second seed is in the southwest corner.

Get them and go to the Smoke Teleporter on the east side (at the edge of the fog, in the center) and enter.

OAK TREE

You will emerge in a new area.

Locate two more seeds on the ground and go to the Circle of Stones with an oak tree in the center.

Drop the four seeds into the four small stone circles surrounding the Oak Tree.

The Holy Symbol of Ravenkind will appear.

Get the Holy Symbol and return to Ravenloft Castle.

RAVENLOFT CASTLE AGAIN

DUNGEON

Return to the Rooms of Weeping where you used the Blood Bat Key to open the wall and reveal the stairs down.

Descend to the Dungeon.

Follow corridor north and east to the Large Room at end of the corridor.

TELEPORTER

There are many small rooms and three openings in the walls of this area.

You can enter all the rooms except the Locked Central Room.

If you try to enter the opening in the southeast wall, you will be teleported backwards.

BUTTONS

Enter the north opening, go north to the wall and press the button on the north wall.

Enter the east opening, go east to the wall, and press the button on the east wall.

The small locked room in the center will now be open.

Go to it, enter and you will be teleported through the southeast opening.

STRAHD

Have your first character hold the Holy Symbol of Ravenkind.

Head south through door to confront Strahd.

Repeatedly use the Holy Symbol on Strahd until he dies and drops an Amulet.

Get Amulet.

ENDGAME

TRIMIA'S CATALOG

You now possess all the items listed in Trimia's catalog of ingredients to open a Gate and travel out of Ravenloft.

The items are: Red Gem, Elven Crown, Wereraven Feather, Tarokka Card and Lord Dhelt's Holy Symbol (Amulet).

Hold the catalog in one hand and use it to travel to Lord Dhelt and the conclusion of the quest.

ORBS & STUFF

Object	See this Section for Location	Also See Section(s)
Various weapons, etc.	Woods	Location only
Fhalken	Woods	Location only
Various loot	Woods	Location only
Gypsy	Old Svalich Road South	Blood on the Vine Tavern, Potion
Scrolls and books	Burgomaster	Location only
Key to Cavern	Strahd	Cavern
Irmagog	Irmagog	Church Vestibule Key
Jade Cavern Key #1	Gateways	Keys
Jade Cavern Key #2	Keys	More Keys
Jade Cavern Key #3	More Keys	Location only
Jade Cavern Key #4	More Keys	Church Vestibule Key
Church Vestibule Key	Church Vestibule Key	Main Floor
Gold Church Key	Main Floor	Lower Level
Tome of Evil Artifacts	Main Floor	Main Floor Again
Parchment (4)	Lower Level	Main Floor, More Keys
Gold Bones	More Subtleties	Resurrection
Cemetery Key	Main Floor Again	1st Visit to Cemetery
Scroll of Atonement	Church	Werewolf Cave, Albino
Scroll of Cure Disease	Church	Werewolf Cave, Albino
Scroll of Remove Curse	Church	Werewolf Cave, Albino
Bag of Gold Dust (2)	1st, 2nd Visit to Cemetery	Banshee
Bone Vault Key	Barovia (Jeweler's Ghost)	2nd Visit to Cemetery
Rod of Rebirth	2nd Visit to Cemetery	Resurrection
Jeweler's Key	2nd Visit to Cemetery	Red Gem
Elven Tomb Key	Lower Level 2	Location only
Elven Signet	Lower Level 2	Lower Level 2, Elven Crown
Sharp Iron Svalich Road Key	Resurrection	Castle
Tower Key	Castle Levels	Teleporting
Blood Bat Key	Castle Levels	Tarokka Card, Dungeon
Silver Tower Key	Castle Levels	Teleporting
Prisoner	Teleporting	Wereraven Feather
Wereraven Feather	Wereraven Feather	Blood on Vine Tavern, Trimia's Catalog

Blood Key	Werewolf Cave Quest	Location only
Red Gem	Red Gem	Trimia's Catalog
Poison Fog Potion	Blood on the Vine Tavern	Potion
Anodyne Potion	Merchant's Pride	Location only
Ruby Catacomb Key	More Keys	Coins
Forgotten Gold Church Key	More Keys	To Lower Level 2
Sasha's Reading Glass	More Keys	Location only
Sapphire Key	Sapphire Key	Location only
Emerald Key	Emerald Key	Getting Out
Onyx Key	Onyx Key	Getting Out
Coins (15)	Sapphire Key, Onyx Key	Blood on Vine Tavern, Coins, Getting Out, Potion
Sasha's pages (3)	Pages, Reading Glass	Locations only
Teardrop Church Key	Pages	Location only
Seeds of Morninglory (4)	Seeds, Oak Tree	Locations only
Holy Symbol of Ravenkind	Oak Tree	Merchant's Pride, Strahd, Trimia's Catalog
Amulet	Strahd	Strahd, Trimia's Catalog

RETURN TO RINGWORLD

BY
FRED PHILIPP
& CLANCY SHAFFER

TYPE
Animated Adventure

SYSTEM
IBM CD-ROM (Required: 386/25+ MHz, 640K RAM, 2 MB hard disk, 256-color VGA, CD-ROM with minimum 150KB/second transfer rate, MS-DOS 5.0+, Microsoft mouse or 100% compatible with version 6.0 driver in high memory. Supports: Sound Blaster & Pro, Covox Sound Master II, Pro Audio 16, Roland Rap-10)

COMPANY
Tsunami Media

HE SECOND GAME ADAPTED FROM LARRY NIVEN'S SCIENCE FICTION NOVELS, *RETURN TO RINGWORLD* FEATURES THREE CHARACTERS AND LETS YOU SWITCH BETWEEN THEM AT WILL. YOU'LL HAVE TO ASSUME THE ROLE OF QUINN, THE HUMAN MALE, MOST OF THE TIME, BUT OCCASIONALLY MUST WEAR THE BOOTS OF SEEKER, A MEMBER OF THE CAT-LIKE KZIN RACE, OR OF MIRANDA, ANOTHER HUMAN. THE PLOT IS AS CONVOLUTED AS EVER FOR A *RINGWORLD* STORY, A CONSPIRACY IN WHICH THE KZINS, THE PUPPETEERS, A. R. M. AND WHO KNOWS HOW MANY OTHER ALIEN RACES ARE ALL OUT TO GET YOU. (THE OFFICIAL CHARGE IS STEALING A SPACE SHIP, BUT THEY'RE REALLY JUST OUT TO GET YOU.) AS A FUGITIVE FROM EVERY CIVILIZATION IN SPACE, YOU INITIALLY HIDE OUT ON RINGWORLD UNTIL YOU CAN FORM A PLAN FOR PROVING YOUR INNOCENCE. THEN YOU'LL TRAVEL ACROSS SPACE TO

LOCATE THE NECESSARY EQUIPMENT AND INFORMATION. DIGITIZED SPEECH IS HEARD THROUGH-OUT, AND IN FACT THE PROGRAM WON'T EVEN DISPLAY TEXT DESCRIPTIONS WHEN YOU "LOOK" AT THINGS. THE SPEECH AND CINEMATIC SCENES PULL YOU INTO THE STORY, WHOSE PUZZLES ARE MORE CHALLENGING THAN THOSE OF THE FIRST GAME, BUT *RETURN TO RINGWORLD* STILL LOOKS A LOT BETTER THAN IT PLAYS.

THE SOLUTION

LANCE OF TRUTH

BEDROOM

Pick up the stepping disk.
Raise your storage unit and get the stasis gun.
Exit through door.

LAB

Enter lab on the left.
Pick up the tractor unit, reader and sensor probe, then exit.
Take elevator up to the bridge.

BRIDGE

Talk to Seeker and Miranda.
They will tell you that you need to locate the coordinates to travel to Ringworld and that you need to disable the stasis field on the quantum drive.
Give reader to Miranda.

AUTODOC

Go to deck 5.
Move plate on right to get the clamp.

Pull wires on the wall to get the optical fiber.

Enter Sickbay.

Open cabinet and get the Comm Scanner.

Put optical fiber in the autodoc.

Put reader into slot in the autodoc.

Press button on side of the autodoc and lie in autodoc.

Select "advanced procedures" from menu.

Surgery will be performed on Quinn to extract the Info Disk.

COORDINATES

Return to the bridge and give Info Disk to Seeker.

Descend to Landing Bay 2.

LANDING BAY 2

Pick up the cable harness lying on the floor and put it on the wall hook near the door.

Put tractor unit on end of the harness.

Walk to the right and use crane to move overhead magnet around until the cable is attracted to magnet and attached.

VACUUM CHAMBER

Enter door near wall hook.

Open the lockers on left and right to get the sonic blaster and laser diffusion aerosol can.

Pick up O2 TANK on floor, then exit chamber.

Climb up harness to the Engineering Loft.

ENGINEERING LOFT

Enter door and use laser diffusion aerosol can on the laser gun.

Put clamp on the laser gun.

Get aerosol can.

Exit and reenter room.

STASIS FIELD

Use sensor probe on stasis gun to remove spent power capsule.

Use probe on stepping disk to remove powerpack.

Put powerpack in stasis gun.

Look at comm scanner and move tone slider to first setting to the right.

Put scanner on the laser gun.

Shoot at scanner with sonic blaster to dissipate the laser cloud.

Get scanner.

Turn tone off.

Use stasis gun on stasis field.

Go to bridge and speak with Seeker and Miranda to travel to Ringworld.

RINGWORLD

There is much information in the computers scattered around the ship. While not necessary to the solution, it will augment the story line and provide background if you access it.

FIST OF GOD

Use computer on the bridge to scan "deep-active-geographical." Note that the slider bar on the left reflects depth.

To reach the canyon, scan "up" until you see a fractal distortion on the computer screen.

CANYON

Use stasis gun on the attacker, then finish him off with your sonic blaster.

Talk to the dying Chief. (If you played the first *Ringworld,* you'll recognize this Village location.)

The Chief dies, and you return to the ship.

A.R.M. BASE

Use the computer to scan "short range-not active-technological" to locate the A.R.M. Base.

Seeker will ask you what you want to do.

Reply "go back the way we came in" (through the Fist of God.) You will now fly to the Spaceport ledge.

SPACEPORT LEDGE

Go to the Airlock in the Landing Bay.

Push button on the wall to rotate spacesuits until you locate one that fits a human male.

Put the O2 tank on the suit, then wear the suit.

Open airlock.

LEDGE

Walk around awhile until Miranda is captured and your ship is seized.

Use your scanner to scan the ledge (take scanner and place on question mark).

Each symbol on the scanner depicts a location you must visit.

You must locate ten items, then repair a Ledge Hopper.

Keep track of where you've been, because the symbols will remain on the scanner.

SPARE PARTS

You must get these items, which are on the ground: navigational gyro, fuel cell, radar, joystick (Seeker will help you get the joystick).

In the wrecked ship to the southwest, get the airbag and diagnostics display.

In the south-central area, get the Comm Antenna Dish.

Climb up it, lower the dish, and get the guidance control mechanism.

Walk across the arm, open panel and get the battery.

LEDGE HOPPER

Locate the hopper to the west-central area and enter.

Open right panel and get the igniter and valve.

Put joystick in holder.

Open left panel and put diagnostics display in it.

Exit ship.

Put remaining parts (except airbag) from Spare Parts section into empty sockets on ship.

Enter ship and use the joystick to fly up the wall to Rings.

RINGS

Walk north until you locate a Mag-lev Transport Vehicle.

Enter and ride north to the second elevator (a semicircle symbol on the left).

Exit vehicle and go to elevator.

Have Seeker open bottom door.

Have Quinn pull lever inside door.

ROBOT

Go upstairs and enter elevator.

Turn on light.

Use Seeker on Robot to tilt it.

Place airbag under Robot.

Use O2 tank on airbag to topple robot off of elevator.

Hit light switch to raise elevator.

ELEVATOR

Look at Display Screen on side of the elevator.

Push middle button (you will view a cutaway to Miranda and Capt. Teal).

When Teal leaves the room, have Miranda grab the wire on the arm of the chair.

You will be transported to Spill Mountain.

SPILL MOUNTAIN

ARRIVAL

In the cave, talk to the Caretaker; you will be taken to a Chamber with the Leader.

Talk to her to get your next series of quests.

Seeker remains behind while Quinn continues on his own.

BALLOON

Map the mountain.

In cave with the crank, lower rock to the Tanning and Storage cave.

Go to that cave and get a tank.

Continue down to the helium cave and fill the tank with helium (use tank on stopcock).

Go east to Balloon Launch and use tank on the balloon.

The Leader will appear and give you a flute.

Climb in balloon.

IN FLIGHT

Wait, and the balloon will automatically float west, then north, then east to the northeast corner.

When you reach the northeast corner, use the control in the balloon to descend rapidly as possible until you reach the lowest level.

Wait, and the balloon should float south, west, and then north to a river to the desert.

DESERT

Use the scanner to Scan.

Note directional arrow on the scanner, then go in that direction.

Repeat these steps to reach the forest (you'll go south, west, south, east, south, east).

FOREST

Use the flute on Quinn to summon Nej G'Lor, then talk.

Go east to the campfire.

Talk until morning.

When Nej distracts the guard at the outpost, shoot him with the sonic blaster.

You will now get and wear the dead guard's uniform, and Nej will take the body away.

Enter the Outpost and wait.

Your relief will arrive, and you will be flown to a hanger in the A.R.M. Base.

Talk to the guard.

Switch to Seeker.

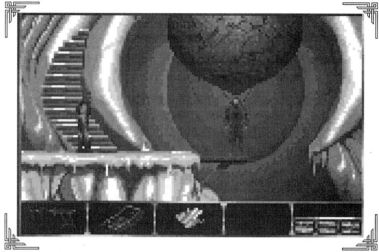

Ballooning will get you everywhere in Ringworld.

SEEKER'S QUEST

Have Seeker go to the cave with the crank and get alcohol.

Check caves below for oil lamp and gunpowder.

Look in another cave for a second oil lamp.

Go to the tanning room for the tanning mask.

In the helium room, get the glass dome.

Go to the room with the crevice above the Balloon Launch.

SCRITH KEY

Click on the rope to untie it, then click on it again to climb down inside crevice.

Put the lamp in the puddle of corrosive fluid.

Put glass dome over lamp.

Pick up the scrith key from the ground, then climb out.

ELEVATOR

Return to the elevator that you first arrived in (all the way up and to the east).

Enter and go down the shaft to the ice that is blocking further progress.

Put gunpowder on ice, then light powder with oil lamp.

Enter the now-exposed opening.

Use alcohol on tanning mask and wear the mask.

Use scrith key to unlock door.

Enter the Vampire's Lair.

VAMPIRE'S LAIR

Kill Vampires with the photon stunner that Seeker is carrying.

You may have to shoot them several times.

GENERAL DIRECTIONS

Go up the first ladder and go all the way east, then down and far to the west.

Go up, down, west, up, east, south and east past two vampires to an area ending in a room to the west.

You'll know you're getting close when told "all the vampires are dead."

PRECISE DIRECTIONS: VAMPIRE'S LAIR

E, U, W, N, E, E, E, U, E, D, E, N, D, W, N, E, N, U, S, U, W, W, W, D, N, D, W, W, U, U, E, S, D, S, E, D, W, W, W, U, N, U, E, S, E, E, E, D, E, N, N, D, W, U, U, W.

(U: up, D: down, E: east, W: west, N: north, S: south. If disoriented, use these directions and sketch a simple map as you go.)

CONTAINMENT FIELD

In the room in the west, you'll find a scroll, a containment field and a keypad.

Get the scroll.

Click on keypad.

Your objective is to turn all sixteen squares pink.

KEYPAD

Click on the square in the northwest corner, then on the squares to the right, right and right.

Drop down to the next row and repeat.

Do the same on the next row down, then on the last row.

This will turn off the containment field, and you will receive the gem.

EXITING

Retrace your steps and find your way out of the Vampire's Lair, up the elevator and out.

Return to the Leader.

Give him the scroll and gem.

Leader will return the Gem of Worlds.

Have Seeker go to the Landing Site Ledge (up from the Balloon Launch) and to the east.

Switch to Miranda.

A.R.M. BASE

BREAKOUT

As Miranda, get pillow.

The jailer should show up to deliver a food tray.

If not, switch back and forth to Seeker and Miranda until he shows up.

Put pillow in the toilet.

Remove bulb from the socket above the toilet.

Insert the wire Miranda got earlier into the socket.

Get the tray the Jailer left and put it on the toilet.

Flush toilet.

Jailer will return and be electrocuted, opening cell bars.

THE GRID

Exit and go left to the Guard's Station.

Pick up the toolbox containing a laser hacksaw.

Return to your cell and use hacksaw on grid to climb up into the Lazer Maze.

LASER MAZE

You must disarm the lasers by rerouting circuits in the laser panels.

This is done by moving three jumpers around to disconnect one or more contact points.

There are 6 contacts.

In the following section, refer to contacts as:

NW N NE

SW S SE

FIRST LASER

Connect one jumper to NW + N.

Connect one jumper to N + NE.

Connect the last jumper to SW + S.

This opens the SE circuit.

Go east to the north-east junction.

Go north to east-west junction.

Go east to the next laser.

SECOND LASER

Move jumpers to: NW + N; N + NE; N + S.

This opens the southwest and southeast contacts.

Go east, then north to north-east junction.

Go east to the next laser.

THIRD LASER

Place jumpers on NW + SW; N + S; N + NE.

This opens the southeast contact.

Go east to the grill.

Look in grill.

Keep looking in grill until the Scientists leave for dinner.

Remove grill and climb through.

GHOULS

Note the Tnuctipun Ship.

Go east into the Anatomy Lab.

Use the computer.

Ghouls will arise and chase you into the hall, where you meet Quinn.

Quinn and Miranda will steal a Hammerhead ship and fly to the ledge on Spill Mountain to rendezvous with Seeker.

PUPPETEER

Webbster, the Puppeteer, will talk to you.

Seeker will show him the Gem of Worlds.

Webbster will tell you that you must enter the Flup Tube at the top of Spill Mountain, descend to the Ocean Floor and fly to the Floating City.

You will then fly into the Flup Tube System.

FLUP TUBE SYSTEM

Go all the way north, west, north, west, and south past the west tube to the end.

Then go east and south to the first tube east to the end.

Go east, then take the first south to the first tube going east.

Go to the end of this tube to enter the Ocean and surface to the Floating City.

FLOATING CITY

Talk to Comrades.

Enter door, then next door to the Outer Walkway.

Walk around Walkway until you find a door leading into the Hub.

Enter room for confrontation with Capt. Teal, who takes the gem.

TELEPORT BEAM

You will all be teleported to the Console room, where Teal places the gem in the console.

A Ghoul soon arrives, kills Teal, enters the Teleport Beam and disappears.

Have Quinn enter the Teleport Beam, and the party will be teleported to the conclusion.

193

ORBS & STUFF

Object	See this Section for Location	Also See Section(s)
Stepping disk	Bedroom	Stasis Field
Stasis gun	Bedroom	Stasis Field, Canyon
Tractor unit	Lab	Landing Bay 2
Reader	Lab	Bridge, Autodoc
Sensor probe	Lab	Stasis Field
Powerpack	Stasis Field	Location only
Navigational gyro	Spare Parts	Ledge Hopper
Fuel cell	Spare Parts	Ledge Hopper
Radar	Spare Parts	Ledge Hopper
Joystick	Spare Parts	Ledge Hopper
Comm Antenna Dish	Spare Parts	Ledge Hopper
Igniter	Ledge Hopper	Location only
Valve	Ledge Hopper	Location only
Wire	Elevator	Breakout
Airbag	Spare Parts	Robot
Diagnostics Display	Spare Parts	Ledge Hopper
Guidance Control Mechanism	Spare Parts	Ledge Hopper
Battery	Spare Parts	Ledge Hopper
Cable harness	Landing Bay 2	Vacuum Chamber
Laser Diffusion Aerosol Can	Vacuum Chamber	Engineering Loft
Spent power capsule	Stasis Field	Location only
Flute	Balloon	Forest
Alcohol	Seeker's Quest	Elevator
Oil lamp (2)	Seeker's Quest	Elevator
Gunpowder	Seeker's Quest	Elevator
Tanning mask	Seeker's Quest	Elevator
Glass dome	Seeker's Quest	Scrith Key
Clamp	Autodoc	Engineering loft
Optical fiber	Autodoc	Location only
Comm Scanner	Autodoc	Stasis field
Info disk	Autodoc	Coordinates
Cable harness	Landing Bay 2	Vacuum Chamber
Spent power capsule	Stasis Field	Location only

194

Flute	Balloon	Forest
Alcohol	Seeker's Quest	Elevator
Oil lamp (2)	Seeker's Quest	Elevator
Gunpowder	Seeker's Quest	Elevator
Tanning mask	Seeker's Quest	Elevator
Glass dome	Seeker's Quest	Scrith Key
Scrith key	Scrith key	Elevator
Photon stunner	Vampire's Lair	Location only
Scroll	Containment Field	Exiting
Gem	Keypad	Exiting
Gem of Worlds	Exiting	Puppeteer
Pillow	Breakout	Location only
Bulb	Breakout	Location only
Tray	Breakout	Location only
Toolbox	The Grid	Location only
Laser hacksaw	The Grid	Location only

SUPERHERO LEAGUE OF HOBOKEN

BY
PAUL SHAFFER

TYPE
Animated Adventure & Role-playing

SYSTEM
IBM PC & CD-ROM (Required: 386/20+, hard disk, 2 MB RAM, DOS 5.)+, Microsoft-compatible mouse, VGA. Supports: Ad Lib, Roland MT-32/LAPC with MPU-401 compatible interface, Sound Blaster)

COMPANY
Legend Entertainment

STEVE MERETZKY'S FIRST FORAY INTO THE REALM OF ROLE-PLAYING, *SUPERHERO LEAGUE* TAKES PLACE TWO CENTURIES IN THE FUTURE, WHEN RADIATION AND TOXIC WASTE HAVE SPAWNED MILLIONS OF MUTANTS AND PLUNGED THE WORLD INTO A NEW DARK AGE. AFTER CHOOSING PARTY MEMBERS SUCH AS MADEMOISELLE PEPPERONI (WHOSE SUPER POWER ENABLES HER TO SEE INSIDE PIZZA BOXES), YOU EMBARK ON A SERIES OF MISSIONS TO RESTORE CIVILIZATION. ULTIMATELY, THIS MEANS DEFEATING THE EVIL VILLAIN, DR. ENTROPY, WHO LIKES THINGS THE WAY THEY ARE. INDOOR SCENES AND LOGICAL PUZZLES ARE PRESENTED IN THE SAME STYLE AS LEGEND ENTERTAINMENT'S PREVIOUS ADVENTURES, WITH A POINT AND CLICK INTERFACE AND EASY-TO-USE ICONS. OUTDOORS, THE PARTY IS REPRESENTED BY A GLOWING ORB ON AN AERIAL-VIEW MAP. COMBAT SCENES ARE TREATED AS IN *WIZARDRY*.

SOUND EFFECTS AND MUSIC SET THE MOOD THROUGHOUT, AND THE CD VERSION FEATURES VOICES.

WHILE THIS IS MAINLY A PARODY OF COMIC BOOK SUPERHEROES, MERETZKY SATIRIZES ROLE-PLAYING AND ADVENTURE GAMES TOO. INSTEAD OF FACING WIZARDS IN COMBAT, YOU'LL FIGHT LAWYERS WHO ISSUE INJUNCTIONS RATHER THAN CAST SPELLS. THE MORE YOU'VE PLAYED THESE KINDS OF GAMES, THE MORE YOU'LL ENJOY HOBOKEN,. BUT MERETZKY'S MAIN TARGET IN THIS PARODY — SUPERHEROES — GIVES *SUPERHERO LEAGUE OF HOBOKEN* UNIVERSAL APPEAL.

THE SOLUTION

GENERAL

To reach some locations, you must cross water, which requires having Treader Man and any other member who has drunk the aqua isotope (from the HQ storage cabinet) in your party. Crossing deep water requires having three party members with Tread Water ability of at least 50%. Before you're able to cross water, you should be able to find ferries across most large bodies of water.

Missions in each level may be accomplished in any order. After completing a mission, return to HQ to rest and refill food supplies, since returning sometimes activates new necessary sequences. Each time you start a new level, listen to the chatterbox in the HQ computer room for hints. Also revisit pawnbroker shops after attaining a higher level, as they may stock new items. Use color-coded tube passes on correspondingly colored tubes.

COMBAT TIPS

"Raise cholesterol" and "put animals to sleep" work only on living opponents. For any machine-related enemy, use "induce rust." For any plant attacker, use "induce root rot." There seems to be a tendency for an attack to fail if the same attack is used consecutively on the same enemy.

LEVEL ONE

JALAPENO PEPPERS

With Iron Tummy in the party, go to Sector 2C;6, 8 and enter downtown Newark.
Go to the warehouse at 10, 2.

Use Iron Tummy's "Eat spicy food" ability on peppers.

Take rag.

THE LIMBURGER BOMB

Go to the Paterson pawnbroker (Section 2D;8, 8) and buy cheese-eating microbes.

Go to the Jersey City village (Section 2C;12, 8) and open Hyundai trunk.

Pour cheese-eating microbes on bomb.

Use rag on transmission fluid.

RABID SHEEP

Go to the Paterson pawnbroker (Section 2D;8, 8) and buy sheep spray.

Go to East Orange Village (Section 2C;7.11) and spray sheep.

Use rag on sheep drool.

COMPUTER WORSHIP

Go to Paterson Temple (Sector 2D;7, 10).

Break the pot.

Use rag on dirt left by broken pot.

Also take the greeting card, the plant and the magnet.

ENTROPY'S LAB

With Robomop in party, go to Edison's lab (Sector 2C;4, 12).

Read warranty.

Use rag on plating.

Enter secret room and use Robomop's ability to clean the mess.

Unplug the power cord.

Take 100-watt bulb and cone from phonograph.

LEVEL TWO

SILLY PUTTY

Get gray tubecar pass from storage cabinet at HQ.

Go to the Newark Control Tower (Sector 2C;7, 6) and open the locker, taking Pappy outfit.

Go to Hackensack village (Sector 2D;13, 6) and enter the shaman's tent.

Wear outfit and talk to the dying man.

Remove outfit and talk to dying man again.

Take plastic egg.

SCRANTON LEAGUE

With Madamoiselle Pepperoni, go to downtown Newark and enter the Tram (9, 10).

Take the gray tram to Scranton and get the Bowdlerizer ray gun in the tram station.

Go to Scranton League HQ (6, 5) and have Pepperoni fire the Bowdlerizer ray gun.

Take the lump of coal.

PISCATAWAY WARLORD

Go to the Piscataway warlord (Sector 1B;13, 9).

Take bust off shelf.

Put magnet (from inventory) on shelf.

Wait for magnet to remove toupee, then take the paperweight.

GUACAMOLE

Go to Sector 1C;4, 5.

Remove the light panel and take the 98-watt bulb.

Put the 100-watt bulb (from inventory) in the socket.

Take guacamole and avocado.

ENTROPY'S PIGEONS

Return to your HQ and go to the basement.

200

Open Sinatra statue and take DAT tape.

Go to the Piscataway pawnbroker (Sector 1B;12, 7) and buy transmitter.

Open transmitter and put in DAT tape.

Close transmitter and go to the Newark Control Tower (Sector 2C;7, 6).

Attempt to go up stairs.

Give avocado, plastic egg, paperweight and lump of coal to Collector.

Go up to face Entropy.

Turn transmitter on.

Spells don't work as well when used consecutively on the same foe .

LEVEL THREE

MINEOLA RADIATION TROUBLE

Go to Yonkers Village (Sector 3D;6, 9) and buy longjohns from the pawnbroker.

Go to Mineola Village (Sector 4C;1.9).

You will be rewarded for this mission with a turnstile token.

WASHINGTON MUSEUM

Go to the Paterson Warlord (Sector 2D;9, 9).

Take the plastic case, the fur coat and the coat rack.

Go to the Washington Museum (Sector 1C;9, 12) and put rack on the spot on floor.

Take uniform, wig and false teeth.

You will be rewarded for this mission with a turnstile token.

CORRUPT PRIESTS

Go to Piscataway village (Sector 1B;12, 7) and buy wire cutters from pawnbroker.

Go to the Piscataway temple (Sector 1B;11, 7) and hide under altar.

Wait until you see priest's shoe appear.

Examine knot and take loose board.

Cut wire with wire cutters and leave hiding place.

Wait and watch priest's scam be discovered.

You will be rewarded for this mission with a turnstile token.

LIBERTY BELL

Go to Yonkers Village (Sector 3D;6, 9).

Give plastic case (from inventory) to shaman (getting NO2 canister).

Buy orienteering guide while you're there.

In a random fight about this time you should be getting a red tubecar pass.

Go to the Newark tram station and take the plastic tubing.

Use the red tubecar to get to Philadelphia.

Go to 14, 8 and agree to work out.

Go to the Liberty Bell (10, 6) and put plastic tubing in bell's crack.

Use NO2 canister on plastic tube.

Shake NO2 canister.

Lift the bell and take the whistle.

You will be rewarded for this mission with a turnstile token.

ENTROPY'S BREEDING SCHEME

Go to Bernardsville Village (Sector 1C;5, 8) and take placard.

Go to Belmont Park (Sector 3C;13, 7) and put placard on steel frame. (In order to reach Belmont Park, you must have all four turnstile tokens from the previous four missions.)

Take green tubecar pass.

LEVEL FOUR

TIMES SQUARE

Go to Yankee Stadium (Sector 3D;3, 2) and pour aluminum eating-microbes (from inventory) on strongbox.

Take ball and go to the seawall (Sector 3C;1, 10).

Enter seawall and proceed to Times Square in Downtown New York (3, 9).

Give ball to Dick Clark.

Take the ochre bedistor.

Go to Grand Central Station (10, 8) and take yellow tubecar pass.

YALE VS. PRINCETON

Go to New Haven by entering the Empire State Building in Downtown New York (7, 3), and going down.

Take the green tubecar and go to Yale's campus (8, 3).

Go to the Science Museum (2, 9) and enter exhibit room.

Take termite hatchery, banana and washing machine.

Go west.

Put the washing machine on either spot, then stand on the other one.

Wait for Yale guys to come, and you'll overhear their plan.

Go to the Princeton Library (Sector 1A;1, 9) and talk to the coach.

Take the maroon bedistor.

FLUSHING LEAGUE

Go to Shea Stadium (Sector 3C;7, 10) and blow the whistle (inventory).

Take the mouse carcass and the bedistor.

PHILADELPHIA SEWERS

Go to Philadelphia (7, 1).

Enter sewers and work your way to 16, 1 (getting diet book and bedistor).

ENTROPY AT YANKEE STADIUM

Go to Yonkers Village (Sector 3D;6, 9) and buy purple tubecar pass from pawnbroker.

Go to Yonkers tram (Sector 3D;5, 10) and take purple tubecar to Poughkeepsie.

Go to 12, 2, where you're given a metal rod and computer printout.

Read computer printout.

Go to Uptown New York and enter the vault (15, 5).

Use metal rod in hole of the fourth booth.

Take frozen body.

Return to Yankee Stadium.

Open the booth.

Put frozen body in booth.

Close booth.

Put each bedistor in its correspondingly colored socket.

Push the button.

Open the booth.

LEVEL FIVE

POUGHKEEPSIE WARLORD

Go to the Poughkeepsie Warlord (16, 7).

North.

Wear the George Washington uniform, wig and false teeth (inventory).

Speak with the warlord and talk him out of invading (getting poker chip).

UNCOMPLIANT SHAMAN

Go to Philadelphia and enter Ben Franklin's place (6, 5).

Free King Midas by winning battle.

Return to HQ and get Midas to join the party.

Go to Freehold Village (Sector 2A;2, 4) and talk to shaman.

Talk to merchant in weapon shop.

Talk to innkeeper at inn.

Talk to madam in brothel.

Talk to shaman again.

Talk to madam (asks you for something warm).

Give fur coat (inventory) to madam.

Use Midas on any previously used inventory items (mouse carcass, teeth, uniform).

Do this twice to get a muffler/scarf.

Give scarf to madam, who then gives you a rate sheet.

Return to inn and show rate sheet to innkeeper.

Return to weapon shop and show sheet to merchant.

Return to shaman and show sheet to him.

Return to HQ (getting poker chip).

NEW YORK TRIBAL WAR

Go to the cave at New Haven (7, 12) and take music sheet.

Practice sheet (you are taken to Carnegie Music Hall).

Sit at piano.

Play piano.

Take sandbag.

Open sandbag, taking both totems.

Enter light.

Go to Radio City Music Hall in Downtown New York (5, 12).

Give rah kett totem to rah kett leader.

Go to the UN Building (16, 9) and give yu wen totem to yu wen leader (getting poker chip).

RECOVERING VIDEOTAPE

Go to the Huntington warlord (Sector 4D;12, 6) and examine table.

Take videotape.

Go to the Princeton Library (Sector 1A;1, 9) and give videotape to curator (getting poker chip).

ENTROPY'S TREE

Go to Princeton Village (Sector 1A;1, 10) and buy termite eggs from pawnbroker.

Go to Staten Island Village (Sector 2B;8, 10) and buy orange tubepass from pawnbroker.

Take orange tubecar at Philadelphia tram to Atlantic City.

Go to Trump casino (4, 4).

Put all four poker chips (inventory) into slot in slot machine.

Enter secret passage.

Open termite hatchery (inventory).

Put termite eggs in hatchery.

Close it, turn it on and then open it.

LEVEL SIX

MAP OVERLOAD

With Glovebox in your party, go to Staten Island Village (Sector 2B;8, 10).

Enter inn and use Glovebox's power to refold the maps.

Take beer.

SCRANTON TEMPLE

Go to Atlantic City.

Go to the vault (15, 9), obtaining the pez dispenser and Enquirers.

Go to Scranton.

Go to the Scranton Temple (1, 10) and examine stain.

Go to Scranton Village (4, 11) and put Enquirers (inventory) in newspaper basket.

Wait for the paperboy (getting mushroom soup).

ALLIGATORS IN THE SEWERS

Go to Uptown New York.

Enter the sewers at 12, 7.

Go to all five dead end alleys in sewers (killing alligators) and get alligator droppings.

THREE MILE ISLAND

Go to Staten Island Village (Sector 2B;8, 10) and buy silver tubepass from pawnbroker.

Return to New York sewers and enter tram station in sewer center (getting gum).

Go to Philadelphia tram (using the brown tubecar pass, which you should already have obtained after a random fight).

Take the silver tubecar to Harrisburg..

A fight here will gain you a paperclip.

Go to Three Mile Island (15, 2).

Open deactivation unit.

Use paper clip (inventory) on electrodes.

Pull lever.

Use chewing gum on hole.

Pull lever.

Take uranium pellet.

ENTROPY

Go to the Statue of Liberty (Sector 2C;13, 6).

Take the robot manual and read it.

Attempt to go up.

Open beer can.

Put uranium pellet in beer.

Put alligator dropping in beer.

Put the cone in the beer, then put the mushroom soup into the cone.

Give beer to android.

Go upstairs.

LEVEL SEVEN

ENDGAME

With Mighty Magnitude in your party, go to Harrisburg Village (9, 4) and take the master tubecar pass.

Go to Scranton and enter pit (15, 9).

Have Magnitude use his powers on the bananas three times.

Take the bananas.

Go to Buffalo, using the gold tubecar in the Scranton tram.

Go to Chippawa Village (4, 9) and buy the blanc isotope from the pawnbroker.

Go to Chippawa warlord (1, 6) and Tonawanda warlord (16, 8) and listen to conversation.

Go to the rest station (12, 1) and have a member of the party drink the blanc isotope.

Use Magnitude's "Power of 10" on the tree.

Use the new "Beaver Jaw" ability on the tree.

Go to the falls (3, 11), getting barrel.

Go to 7, 7, obtaining the plowshare and hook.

Go to the farm (7, 6).

Give barrel, plowshare and hook to farmer, getting the key.

Go to the Empire State Building in Downtown New York (7, 3).

Push elevator call button.

Enter elevator (takes you to Entropy).

Use Magnitude's "Power of 10" on bananas three times.

Turn off the projector.

ORBS & STUFF

Due to the exacting nature of this game, the objects table varies slightly from the others by providing precise locations of each object rather than referring you to a section of the solution.

Object	See this Section for Location	Also See Section(s)
	LEVEL ONE	
Aqua isotope	Storage cabinet at HQ	General
Blue tubecar pass	Storage cabinet at HQ	General
Aluminum-eating microbes	Storage cabinet at HQ	Times Square
Oil-eating microbes	Storage cabinet at HQ	Not used
Rag	Warehouse (Downtown Newark; 10, 2)	Limburger Bomb, Rabid Sheep, Entropy's Lab
Cheese-eating Microbes	Paterson pawnbroker (Sector 2D;8, 8)	Limburger Bomb
Sheep spray	Paterson pawnbroker (Sector 2D;8, 8)	Rabid Sheep
Transmission fluid	Jersey city village (Sector 2C;12, 8)	Limburger Bomb
Sheep drool	East Orange village (Sector 2C;7, 11)	Rabid Sheep
Pot	Paterson temple (Sector 2D;7, 10)	Computer Worship
Dirt	Paterson temple (Sector 2D;7, 10)	Computer Worship
Plant	Paterson temple (Sector 2D;7, 10)	Computer Worship
Magnet	Paterson temple (Sector 2D;7, 10)	Computer Worship, Piscataway Warlord
Greeting card	Paterson temple (Sector 2D;7, 10)	Computer Worship
Warranty	Edison's lab (Sector 2C;4, 12)	Entropy's Lab
100-watt bulb	Edison's lab (Sector 2C;4, 12)	Entropy's Lab, Guacamole
Cone	Edison's lab (Sector 2C;4, 12)	Entropy's Lab, Entropy
	LEVEL TWO	
Gray tubecar pass	HQ storage cabinet	Silly Putty, Scranton League
Pappy outfit	Newark Control Tower (Sector 2C;7, 6)	Silly Putty
Plastic egg	Hackensack village (Sector 2D;13, 6)	Silly Putty, Entropy's Pigeons
Bowdlerizer ray gun	Scranton tram station (11, 8)	Scranton League
Lump of coal	Scranton League HQ (6, 5)	Scranton League, Entropy's Pigeons
Bust	Piscataway warlord (Sector 1B;13, 9)	Piscataway Warlord
Paperweight	Piscataway warlord (Sector 1B;13, 9)	Entropy's Pigeon

Light panel	Guacamole factory (Sector 1C;4, 5)	Guacamole
98-watt bulb	Guacamole factory (Sector 1C;4, 5)	Guacamole
Guacamole	Guacamole factory (Sector 1C;4, 5)	Guacamole
Avocado	Guacamole factory (Sector 1C;4, 5)	Guacamole, Entropy's Pigeon
DAT tape	HQ basement (Sector 2C;13, 9)	Entropy's Pigeons
Transmitter	Piscataway village (Sector 1B;12, 7)	Entropy's Pigeons

LEVEL THREE

Lead-lined longjohns	Yonkers village (Sector 3D;6, 9)	Mineoloa Radiation Trouble
Plastic case	Paterson warlord (Sector 2D;9, 9)	Washington Museum, Liberty Bell
Fur coat	Paterson warlord (Sector 2D;9, 9)	Washington Museum, Uncompliant Shaman
Coat rack	Paterson warlord (Sector 2D;9, 9)	Washington Museum, Uncompliant Shaman
Uniform	Washington museum (Sector 1C;9, 12)	Washington Museum, Poughkeepsie Warlord
Wig	Washington museum (Sector 1C;9, 12)	Washington Museum, Poughkeepsie Warlord
False teeth	Washington museum (Sector 1C;9, 12)	Washington Museum, Poughkeepsie Warlord
Wire cutters	Piscataway village (Sector 1B;12, 7)	Corrupt Priests
Loose board	Piscataway temple (Sector 1B;11, 7)	Corrupt Priests
NO2 canister	Yonkers village (Sector 3D;6, 9)	Liberty Bell
Orienteering guide	Yonkers village (Sector 3D;6, 9)	Liberty Bell
Red tubecar pass	Random fight	Liberty Bell
Plastic tubing	Newark tram station (9, 10)	Liberty Bell
Whistle	Liberty Bell (Philadelphia;10, 6)	Liberty Bell, Yale vs. Princeton
Placard	Bernardsville village (Sector 1C;5, 8)	Entropy's Breeding Scheme
Green tubecar pass	Belmont Park (Sector 3C;13, 7)	Entropy's Breeding Scheme, Yale vs. Princeton

LEVEL FOUR

Strange ball	Yankee Stadium (Sector 3D;3, 2)	Times Square
Yellow tubecar pass	Grand Central (Downtown NY;10, 8)	Times Square
Ochre bedistor	Times Square (Downtown NY;3, 9)	Entropy at Yankee Stadium
Termite hatchery	Museum of Science (New Haven;2, 9)	Yale vs. Princeton, Entropy's Tree
Banana	Museum of Science (New Haven;2, 9)	Yale vs. Princeton

Washing machine	Museum of Science (New Haven;2, 9)	Yale vs. Princeton
Maroon bedistor	Princeton Library (Sector 1A;1, 9)	Entropy at Yankee Stadium
Mouse carcass	Shea Stadium (Sector 3C;7, 10)	General
Ecru bedistor	Shea Stadium (Sector 3C;7, 10)	Entropy at Yankee Stadium
Mauve bedistor	Philadelphia sewers (16, 1)	Entropy at Yankee Stadium
Diet book	Philadelphia sewers (16, 1)	Philadelphia Sewers
Purple tubecar pass	Yonkers village (Sector 3D;6, 9)	Entropy at Yankee Stadium
Metal rod	Poughkeepsie (12, 2)	Entropy at Yankee Stadium
Computer printout	Poughkeepsie (12, 2)	Entropy at Yankee Stadium
Frozen body	Vault (Uptown NY;15, 5)	Entropy at Yankee Stadium

LEVEL FIVE

Poker chip	Poughkeepsie warlord (16, 7)	Poughkeepsie Warlord, Entropy's Tree
Poker chip	HQ (after completing Freehold mission)	Entropy's Tree
Poker chip	UN Building or Radio City	Entropy's Tree
Poker chip	Princeton library (Sector 1A;1, 9)	Entropy's Tree
Muffler/scarf	Made by King Midas ability	Uncompliant Shaman
Rate sheet	Freehold Village (Sector 2A;2, 4)	Uncompliant Shaman
Music sheet	Cave (New Haven;7, 12)	New York Tribal War
Sandbag	Carnegie Hall	New York Tribal War
Yu wen totem	Carnegie Hall	New York Tribal War
Rah kett totem	Carnegie Hall	New York Tribal War
Videotape	Huntington warlord (Sector 4D;12, 6)	Recovering Videotape
Termite eggs	Princeton village (Sector 1A;1, 10)	Entropy's Tree
Orange tubecar pass	Staten Island village (Sector 2B;8, 10)	Entropy's Tree

LEVEL SIX

Beer	Staten Island village (Sector 2B;8, 10)	
Silver tubecar pass	Staten Island village (Sector 2B;8, 10)	
Pez dispenser	Vault (Atlantic City;15, 9)	Scranton Temple
National Enquirers	Vault (Atlantic City;15, 9)	Scranton Temple
Mushroom soup	Scranton village (4, 11)	Scranton Temple, Entropy
Alligator dropping	Sewers (Uptown NY;12, 7)	Entropy
Brown tubecar pass	Random fight	Three Mile Island
Paperclip	Harrisburg (random fight)	Three Mile Island

Chewing gum	Tram (Philadelphia;7, 1)	Three Mile Island
Turnstile tokes (4)	Complete first four missions in Level Three	Entropy's Breeding Scheme
Uranium pellet	Three-Mile Island (Harrisburg;15, 2)	Entropy
Robot manual	Statue of Liberty (Sector 2C;13, 6)	Entropy

LEVEL SEVEN

Master tubecar pass	Harrisburg village (9, 4)	Endgame
Bananas	Pit (Scranton;15, 9)	Endgame
Blanc isotope	Chippawa Village (Buffalo;4, 9)	Endgame
Barrel	Niagara Falls (Buffalo;3, 11)	Endgame
Plowshare	Buffalo (7, 7)	Endgame
Hook	Buffalo (7, 7)	Endgame
Empire State elevator key	Farm (Buffalo;7, 6)	Endgame

ULTIMA VIII: PAGAN

BY
CLANCY SHAFFER
& FRED PHILIPP

TYPE
Fantasy Role-playing

SYSTEM
IBM (Required: 486/33+, 4 MB RAM, VGA, DOS 5.0+, 35 MB hard disk (CD version also installs to and plays from hard disk), 100% Microsoft-compatible mouse. Supports: General MIDI, Ad Lib, Sound Blaster & compatibles (Sound Blaster or compatible required for digitized speech and sounds. Recommended: 486/50+, 8 MB RAM)

COMPANY
Origin, Inc.

213

HE LATEST INSTALLMENT IN LORD BRITISH'S SERIES TAKES PLACE IMMEDIATELY AFTER SERPENT ISLE (ULTIMA 7, PART 2). AT THE END OF THAT QUEST, THE EVIL GUARDIAN SNATCHED UP THE AVATAR AND STRANDED HIM ON THE WORLD OF PAGAN. AS THE AVATAR, YOU STRIVE TO ESCAPE THIS, THE FIRST OF MANY WORLDS CONQUERED BY THE GUARDIAN, WHICH INVOLVES DEFEATING THE FOUR TITANS OF POWER. THE WEAKEST GAME IN THE ULTIMA SERIES, PAGAN ENDOWS THE AVATAR WITH ARCADE-STYLE ABILITIES SUCH AS JUMPING AND CLIMBING, WHICH LEADS TO AN OVER-ABUNDANCE OF NINTENDO-TYPE PUZZLES THAT CONFLICT WITH ULTIMA'S ESSENTIAL ROLE-PLAYING NATURE. THE PERSPECTIVE OF THE OVERHEAD GRAPHICS, BY PLACING NORTH AT THE UPPER RIGHT CORNER OF THE SCREEN RATHER THAN AT THE TOP, IS ALSO DISORIENTING. THE MAGIC SYSTEM, CENTERING ON EARTH, AIR, FIRE AND

WATER ELEMENTALS AND INVOLVING THE USE OF REAGENTS, IS THE ONLY INTERESTING ASPECT OF THE GAME. INTERACTING WITH THE CITIZENS OF PAGAN AND SLAYING MONSTER AFTER MONSTER ARE FUN ACTIVITIES, BUT JUMPING AND CLIMBING ACROSS LEVEL AFTER LEVEL ARE NOT FOR MOST ROLE-PLAYERS.

THE SOLUTION

GENERAL

Directions are confusing, due to a game design that places north in the upper right-hand corner of the screen. You can jump only in the eight cardinal points of the compass. The secret of jumping is to line up with your directional arrows and save the game. If you jump incorrectly, restore and back up a little for your next jump. After you learn sorcery, you can cast the Flash spell to reach inaccessible spaces. You will need to have 250 coins by the end of the game. The Thamaturgical spells Mythran spells are not necessary for finishing the game, and it is not necessary to kill most of the monsters. If you're having trouble killing a particular creature, just run around it.

EXPLORING TENEBRAE

In the beginning, look in the two barrels for a dagger.

Get the bedroll and other items that Devon leaves by the fireside.

Armor, a dagger and a keyring can be found in the guard posts around the castle (if the doors to the posts are locked, climb the walls).

Climb the castle walls and go to the teleport square on the middle of the roof, walking over it in order to activate it.

At the Blacksmith in West Tenebrae, wait until he leaves, and you can steal a sword and perhaps some armor.

THE MAGE MYTHRAN

To find the Mage, follow the path that exits the castle to the north (heading N/NW) and leads into a tunnel in the mountains.

You will encounter ghouls in the tunnel and must cross water to reach the Mage's home (jumping across the stones).

Save the game before your first jump, and save again after every successful jump.

As you go further through the tunnel, you will see a windlass.

Past that (over a bridge) is a wrecked building.

Go to the building and move the three levers on the top of the screen against the wall, and the three lower levers away from the wall (don't use the lever in the center of the room, which resets the puzzle).

If you think an earthquake is occurring, you know you did it right.

Return to the windlass and use the lever (opens the gates).

Continue south through the gates, and you will exit the tunnel.

Outside, proceed south to find the Mage in his house. He will give you a Recall disk that you can use to return to Tenebrae (if you activated the teleport there).

Before leaving, activate the teleport square on the upper floor of the house in order to return here later.

THE CEMETERY

Go to East Tenebrae and continue east until you find the exit in the east wall.

Exit East Tenebrae and follow the wall north to another exit in the north wall.

Exit to the cemetery and follow the path to a gate.

Enter the gate and the building behind it.

Talk to Vividos, asking to join the Necromancers.

THE CEREMONIAL DAGGER

After your conversation with Vividos on the second floor, leave and return to the Castle.

If the Queen is eating, you can enter the Throne room.

Under the pad on the small table is a pillow.

Look under the pillow and get the key, which opens the bedroom door.

Enter the bedroom and speak to Arimina, the Queen's lady in waiting, who will tell you to meet her during Bloodwatch.

Note the time on the clock on the table in the Throne Room: sleep until Bloodwatch, then go to East Tenebrae.

When you enter East Tenebrae, turn right (the Avatar's right) and follow this road until you see four large pools of water on your left.

Go east between the pools until you see a house with double doors on your left and a fence on your right.

If it's Bloodwatch, the house will be unlocked (sometimes it takes a few minutes).

Enter and insist upon an answer.

Say "Are you certain," and she will give you the key.

Enter the Queen's bedroom while she is eating.

Use the key you got from the table, then use the key from Arimina on the closet door and the chest.

Take the dagger (in the small chest) and the invisibility scroll.

Take the dagger back to Vividos and save before you enter the building.

NECROMANCER'S INITIATION

Enter and agree to take part in the Necromancer's ceremony.

After the ceremony, you will be told that Vividos is the new Necromancer and you are his apprentice.

He sends you to get some special sticks from an old haunted house that is in West Tenebrae, situated a little left of the Pits where the Trolls fight.

The sticks are things that resemble a Y and are stacked against a tree in one corner of the house: get them quickly, or you will be attacked by Ghouls and a Ghost.

MONKS' HOODS

Exit the cemetery (outside of east Tenebrae).

Follow the east wall down to the water, then move a bit to your west.

You'll see a pit with crude stairs going down. In the center are black flowers; these are the Monks' Hoods.

Attack the mimics, then jump on the mound in the center.

Get the Hoods and return to Vivados.

Vivados will send you to the second story to study.

Take the items and the bag there.

The bag already contains the ingredients to cast the Wall spell.

HALL OF CANDLES: LEARNING SPELLS

In order to cast Necromantic spells, you must put the necessary reagents into a pouch.

Set the pouch on the ground and click on it.

After obtaining the above items, return to Vivados.

He tells you to cast the Open Ground spell in the hall to the north; you must go outside the building, through the fence, then north to a new building.

Run from the monsters to the side of the building and enter the Hall of Candles.

Go up the middle isle to the rock wall, cast your spell and enter.

Run from the Skeleton Guard.

DEATH MASK: FIRST TRIAL

Push the center lever to get through the gate, then push the lever on your side to close it.

Wander around until you see a crypt in the open with a jewel box and body in it.

The spider web conceals a door.

Before entering, make sure you have enough ingredients for at least four Dead Speak spells.

Open the door, and the floor will open and drop you down into the next level.

When you meet the first Necromancer, cast Dead Speak on him, and he will teach you the spell of Death Mask.

ROCK FLESH: SECOND TRIAL

When you encounter three demons and a Kith, cast Death Mask and wait until they leave.

Go to your left, and you will find a Necromancer who will teach you the Rock Flesh spell.

SUMMON DEAD & GRANT PEACE: TRIALS 3 & 4

As you progress, you will run into Lightning and must use the Rock Flesh spell to get through.

Collect reagents as you go

The next Necromancer will teach you the Summon Dead spell.

You must pass through a sparking fence, then jump across a gully.

Prepare your Summon Dead and Dead Speak spells.

If you move to the Necromancer quickly and cast Dead Speak on him, you will probably not have to fight several Skeleton Warriors and several Ghouls.

The Necromancer will teach you Grant Peace.

When you finish speaking, you are teleported to an area of trees and grass.

WITHSTAND DEATH: FIFTH TRIAL

North of here are some splintered bones.

Move the candles and open the chests for more components.

As you enter the room containing the stone chair, you are teleported to another dungeon.

When you see something like a palace portico, go up and get the gear there, which includes Magic Armor and some components.

Cast Rock Flesh and go north.

Work your way out on a point and jump from there to the plateau just south.

You jump over and land in crevice, where you must defeat a Kith.

Go in the direction that appears northeast on the screen, and check the dead man for leggings and a helmet.

The fifth Necromancer will tell you that the next one will give you something that will let you visit Lithos the Mountain King.

At once you are transported to another place and taught the Withstand Death spell, which can be used only once.

CREATE GOLEM: SIXTH TRIAL

After a harrowing journey through explosions and falling rocks, you will find the sixth Necromancer.

He teaches you Create Golem and tells you to go to Stone Cove.

Ascend the steps next to the Crypt to return to the catacombs (casting Grant Peace on the Ghost if necessary).

THE SLAYER

To get a good weapon, return to the Guard House outside of East Tenebrae.

Instead of going north back to the cemetery, follow the road south (it quickly dead ends) ,turn to your left and go across the grass to a house that has a skeleton on the floor.

Enter the house and drop through the floor.

You land in a room with a Troll, who won't attack if you don't bother him.

Get the key from the trunk in the corner, then read the book.

Leave the room and head south and west until you run into a Platform with a book on it.

You can climb up by standing on the corpse on the near side.

Check the bodies, then read the book.

Continue in a westerly direction until you see a room with peasant women inside.

As you enter, you will face a Troll.

Save the game before fighting the Troll, in case you kill one of the peasants.

Get the key.

Go around the corner to another room, but don't enter, as it contains only a dead body.

Now head east and south.

The Skeleton Guards will not bother you if you walk past them.

Read the next book.

Head east from the book, and you will see a booth with a lever in it.

Save the game.

Prepare a Grant Peace spell to use on the Ghost as you throw the lever and open the door.

Go through the door and you will be on a pier.

Line up carefully, save, then jump to the pier north of you.

Jump across, climb the mound in front of you, kill the Ghoul and go to the end of the pier.

Save the game.

Jump to the rock almost due north, then jump to the next one north and again to the next one, and from there to another pier.

You can get gear from many of the bodies on this pier, but save the game first.

You will have to fight a Seeker.

Collect all you can find, then use the key from the Troll's Room to open the door.

Walk around the outer ring to get the lay of the land.

You will see two Skeleton Warriors guarding a door.

When you're ready, go around the building, and they will follow.

Open the door, enter, then close it.

You must jump to the second floor.

Get The Slayer from the shelf at the head of the corpse.

Jump down and go into the building you were standing on.

You will be teleported back to an area near the Cemetery.

The Slayer will kill Ghosts, Demons, Seekers, and the like, but does not kill Warrior Skeletons (the latter revive almost immediately, so you must use Grant Peace on them).

219

SEEKING THE MOUNTAIN KING

Return to the Catacombs.

Search to the north and east for a doorway in the east wall.

Enter the doorway and go south.

Continue south past some empty crypts and look for an opening to the west.

When you reach a barrier, pull the lever on the pier to open it.

Continue south through the door.

Watch for a large rock with the F symbol on it; you will be teleported back here.

South of here you will find a door into a very spacious place, and a double door and a single door just to your east.

Many components may be found here.

After collecting them, go around again and again until you have all you can carry.

Construct a Golem and have him open both doors.

Don't bother about the single door now; it leads to the Pits, which you will hear about later.

INTO THE CASTLE

Enter the large double doors and go north to a ruined castle (from this point on the location of items may be random.)

Crawl inside the castle and push the lever.

Go outside and push the lever, then head south to the first opening west, which is difficult to see.

At this point you will see a lot of red blocks allowing you passage, or you will see a floating bridge of skulls.

Cross this, and you will encounter floating platforms that you must jump across.

Later you will encounter a force field: cast Rock Flesh and run through it.

As you proceed you will have other jumps to make: one seven north, then three northeast.

Save the game on the stone piers to shorten the jumps.

You will arrive at an area with place where you can jump to an island — do not take this, or you will be teleported back to the stone with F on it.

Instead, look for an opening to the west.

Enter this narrow passage, open the trunk and get the key.

Enter the next passage north and use the key on the door.

Inside you will meet the Mountain King; do as he says.

Now if you want to, jump to the island described at the end of the previous section.

You can find some gear there.

Then step on the rock, and you will be teleported to the Caverns (you will encounter another rock before you jump; you may use this instead if you prefer).

Return to the Cemetery, where Vivados will ask you about Lothian's burial.

Go outside the building to the northeast corner and click on Lothian.

All the combat you want in an RPG.

Return to Vivados, who will send you to meet with Morien.

He has given you the Key of Scion, a long staff with a green-eyed skull on top, which is supposed to open locked doors.

You will not meet Morien on this mini-quest, but the key you now have lets you into the rest of the game.

Make the trip back down to the catacombs: the entrance to the Caverns is in the southeast part.

Shortly after you enter, work your way west and south to a blue chapel.

Go to the front door, and you can see some mud inside a wall inside the chapel.

Cast your Golem in this mud and have him open the door or climb the chapel wall.

There are Skeleton Warriors inside, but they will not get inside the wall around the grave.

Cast Open Ground on the grave and get the Heart of the Earth.

THE DECEIVER

If you want the great axe called the Deceiver, go south in the spacious place to the lake.

(If you already have the Slayer, don't bother with the Deceiver.)

Jump across stones to an island and have a Grant Peace spell ready to get rid of the Skeleton Warrior on top of the island.

From here, jump to another island to get the Deceiver.

Continue collecting components on the way back to Vivados.

In the early versions of the program, he may not recognize that you have completed the Pilgrimage; simply proceed past.

THIS WAY TO YOUR FATE

If you have the open secret door spell from Mythran, return to the Catacomb and enter the door that reads "This is the way to your fate" (it's in the northwest section of the Catacombs, near the pavement that has broken through to fire).

The Key of Scion (see Heart of the Earth, above) will open the door.

Go east to the six levers in a closed-in small area.

Save the game.

Push the north lever, and the mesh drops, revealing a trunk (the lever order may vary).

Get the loot.

If you use the levers, don't worry about the pretty balls on the other side of the fence, but don't get caught in the fence trap.

Forget using the steps, for a door just east of them will allow you entry (use a Golem to open it.)

Under these platforms are components including wood, which you will need by now.

Go to the door and open the one with rocks around it (a Golem is also needed here).

Pick up the triangle shield as you enter.

Explore this area completely to find a church.

You have to use a Golem; the small patches of mud will do the trick nicely.

When you find and enter the church there are two sets of doors.

One Golem will open both doors.

Enter the church.

You will find a key under the skeleton on the broken pew.

Put the triangle shield you just found on the Altar, and the three statues will speak to you.

Have a Grant Peace spell ready in your kit and cast Open Secret Door spell on the door behind the statues.

You will be attacked by the spirit of Khumash-Gor: cast Grant Peace on him.

Take the Magic Scimitar and look in the small places for the pyramid-shaped black cone.

When you emerge, the statues will tell you of your future as the greatest Titan — you are to become the Titan of Ether.

THE CATACOMBS' TELEPORT

Explore the rest of the Catacombs.

In one remote corner is a Quake Skull you can use later on the Red cavity at the end of a wall in the Catacombs.

It will blow up the small building next to it, providing another Teleport; you can now teleport to the second floor of the Castle, the Plateau and the Catacombs.

THE DEATH OF MORDEA

Using the Open Secret Door spell, go to the Castle basement and use the spell on the walls of the Evidence Room.

Read the book behind the bars (discovering that Devon is truly the Tempest).

You are automatically escorted to the dock, where Devon is going to be beheaded.

Save the game.

Make the correct statement, and watch Devon defeat Mordea.

MONASTERY OF THEURGY

Now head south in the Caverns.

Just after you pass the gate that you lowered before, go east and you will find a wooden bridge.

Cross it to the Monastery of Theurgy, talk to the people and agree to take two tests.

Always answer the verbal test in a humble fashion.

Most of the answers are as follows, but some may be random: porch, tend, sight, lost battle, remain quite, welcome him home, a weapon destroys, give truthful testimony, comfort, sad.

On the second test, save the game, then stay in the center ring on the Rock.

Walk or jump against the wind.

It will stop soon, and you will have won the test.

Stellos will take over the test and send you to the dungeons below to get silver for your Foci points.

There are a lot of Kith here, so grab eight pieces of silver and get out.

When you find a Stone House without doors, cast Open Secret Door.

Inside is a sword called the "Protector."

After you have eight pieces of silver ore, use the Teleport to reach the Castle.

THE ALTAR OF FOCUS

Find Korack the Smith in the east section by crossing a bridge in the east part of town.

Go north, then follow the road west and south.

Tell Korack to make the Foci.

Once you have the eight Foci pieces, return to the Monastery and place one piece at a time on the top of the Altar of Focus, which will be endowed with power.

Now all you have to do is click on them to make the magic happen.

When you return, Stellos will tell you to go to the cavern below and that you will know what to do.

Go down, but do not go through the door to the silver mine.

Instead, go west to the wounded animal.

Use the Bracer to move him to your side of the water, then cast Restoration to heal him.

THE FOURTH TEST

At this point there is one more test, but it is being delayed until a stolen Foci is recovered.

In order to trigger the fourth test, you must talk to Torwin, Xavier, Cyrus and Stellas.

Then talk to Cyrus again, but this time cast Hear Truth.

He will tell you about Torwin going to Windy Point to conduct an experiment.

To reach Windy Point, go around the Monastery and above the point where you took the Wind Test.

Torwin will give you the stolen Foci, which triggers the fourth test.

At Windy Point, go between the two columns and make a running jump into the void.

You arrive at Pillar 1.

Go northwest to another Pillar, then northeast for three, southeast for one, northeast for two, southeast for one, northeast for one, north for one, northwest for two, southwest for two and northwest for two.

On the second one of these two, you are picked up by Stratos.

Do not ask for Breath of the Wind.

At this point, you will need the magic you have for your next two ventures.

On the last jump when returning, you can invoke Air Walk.

You can use the Recall item anywhere outside of Demon Crag, so teleport to the nearest Teleport.

HYDROS

Look around the entrance to the Monastery to find a second teleport at Carthax Lake.

Leaving the Stratos area, go back into the Caverns and work your way west to a dried-up lake area.

You must search out a bridge that starts across, then stops, but there is a cross-section to which you must jump.

This will take you to the area where Hydros is trapped, which you will recognize by the White Marble.

Get out into the center, and Hydros will appear: agree to free her.

Go back across the bridge and walk along the cliff to a cave in the extreme southwest portion.

Just outside you will see some strange stones.

Enter and either slay the Troll (a Magic weapon is useful), or run through the next exit to avoid it.

In the next cavern, go a little north to a wall with several spikes missing on top.

Climb over at this point, which may take several attempts.

North of this is a wall with a lever that opens part of this wall.

Climb through the opening, and the next gate will open as you approach it.

Look for water and a nearby Grave Marker.

Cast Open Ground on the Grave Marker, freeing Hydros.

THE LAND OF PYROS

Return to the Lake Carthax Teleportal and go back into the Caverns.

Go north through the second sparking doorway, until you see a large Lake of Lava.

You can pass this by going under the cliff overhang on the south.

You will come to a door with levers.

This is a double door; one door replaces the other if you use the levers.

Look carefully, and you will see a switch that will open another door for you.

When you reach a very large Lake of Lava, go to the part that sticks out into the water.

North of where you arrive, a number of tips jut out into the lava: go to the third one to the south and, using the Air spell, jump to the bottom of the screen.

You will land on a piece of rock on the bottom of the cliff-like Island.

A stranger will appear and give you a hint as to where you jump next.

Go along the bottom of the cliff until you reach that point, then climb up and jump south.

If you jump too far, back up a little and try again.

In the east part of Pyros you will find another teleport.

Activate it.

You can teleport back here but you can't teleport out of here.

BANE

Seek out a lady named Bane, who will tell you about Vardoun.

Vardoun wants you to get Bane's secret name.

In order to apprentice you, he will give you his Secret Name.

Use the phrase about "Shrewd Traders," and he will tell you about Bane.

Return to Bane, give her Vardoun's Secret Name, and she kills him and becomes the First Acolyte.

Next she sends you to the Library to study spells, which is rather tricky.

THE LIBRARY

The Pentagram has five points, the top one or the one pointing most to the north, is known as Perivocanae Pa, and shall be considered the number 1 for the purposes of this solution.

Going clockwise are 2 (Mesostalae Pa), 3 (Aphelion), 4 (Mes.-Ze) and 5 (Per.-Ze).

Books in the Library will tell you where to put Red Candles for each of the spells.

Place Black ones on the remaining points — there must be five at all times.

The books will also tell you where to use the reagents, which must be near each of the indicated candles.

A focus, or Foci, is placed in the middle, known as the Locus.

Collect all the Candles and components in the Library, then go to Bane's house and take the Bag and components.

As a Foci, you can use rods, wands, symbols and talismans.

When a Foci is charged but the number of charges is low, you might want to charge it again to raise the number of times it can be used.

Symbols will typically only hold one or two charges.

If you charge an item once, charging it again does not necessarily increase the number of charges it contains.

Talismans are best for summoning and banishing demons.

VADAUN'S HOME

Go to Vadaun's home, where you will find Bane.

Charge the Foci with the spells Endure Heat, Flame Bolt and Flash, making a list by numbers so you don't go wrong.

Put them all in place, then double-click on the Locus.

If you have the correct candles placed but used the wrong reagents, the Avatar will say the correct words and nothing will happen.

If you have the incorrect candles placed, either nothing will happen or the words invoked will be for a different spell.

The Avatar should kneel and intone Sanct Flam or Ort Flam or Flam Por.

You may have to move the regeants around somewhat.

Afterwards, collect all gear but the candles.

Bane will now send you to the Obsidian Castle to meet the master.

THE OBSIDIAN CASTLE

Cast the Intervention spell before entering.

Slay or run from the two demons.

Don't attack the Demon in the next room.

Talk with him, and he will let you use his gear to make additional spells: do so.

Ready Foci with Flash spells, Endure Heat, Armor of Flames and Flame Bolts, then get the candles from the barrel.

After leaving this area, go west, and you'll be teleported to another area.

Take the northeast passage, where you'll encounter three Seekers and lots of explosive fruit.

At the end, you'll also face another Demon.

When you see a large blue symbol, take it quickly and leave to avoid the second Demon.

Cast Flash to get past the rolling Spiked Balls, and Air Walk to jump explosive berries.

You'll need at least five Grant Peace spells to deal with the Warrior Skeletons in the northwest passage or run around them.

At the end is a Lake of Lava.

Make an Endure Heat spell, and you can walk on any lava that has started to harden (it will be brownish).

You follow the logical area along your right, making several jumps.

Save at each jump.

At the end you must climb a cliff and face a Demon.

Cast Intervention and Rock Flesh, and get the next blue symbol.

The four important areas in this area are identified by the name of the spells you need, such as An Flam, Vas Sanct, and so on.

THE MAGE

Just northwest of you is the Mage, who threatens to kill you if you get near him.

Cast Endure Heat, then attack and kill him. Use his gear to make additional spells.

When you enter the Vas Sanct area, you'll need An Flam spells to put out fire.

Go back and make them there, as you will need these in the southwest part of the An Flam area.

In the western section of the An Flam area, you encounter some monsters, but the main problem is to get a Magic Helm and the Symbol out of a magic fire, which requires using An Flam spells.

Extinguish each of the lit points of the pentagram to get to the Symbol.

In the Vas Sanct Area, use Armor Flames against Fire Bolts.

Follow the left wall around to the Symbol and return the same way through this maze.

You will find Magic Armor, Helm and Shield on these four trips.

MALCHIR

When you teleport back, you will need the following spells, or must make them where you find Arcandin: Ignite, Flame Bolt, Explosion, Call Demon and Banish Demon (the latter is a surprise to you is and part of Malchir's test).

Also take one red candle.

Enter the west teleport again, taking you to Malchir, and say you're ready for his tests.

After casting the requested spells, you are transported to an area where Pyros is being called up.

If you have an Ignite spell and the red candle, you will successfully control Pyros — if not, he slays Bane, but is banished by Malchir.

Visit Malchir.

If he attacks by invoking a Demon, cast Flame Armor, Rock Hard Flesh and Intervention, then use the Slayer on the Demon and Malchir.

If you don't have the Slayer, cast Flame Armor and Summon Dead.

Banish Demon if he's called up.

If Malchir casts Flame Shield, be sure that when you Summon Dead they're inside the shield with Malchir or you'll have wasted the spell — let them do your fighting for you.

Before you leave, get the Tongue of Flame from Malchir, which provides three bits of the Blackrock.

If you haven't already, loot Melchir, Bane and Vardoun's quarters (Melchir's staff should make a great Foci).

With the Tongue of Flame, walk across the large Pentagram near the Library, freeing Pyros; raining fire indicates this has been accomplished.

RETURN TO THE CAVERNS

If you're having problems getting back across the lava, use Air Walk and jump (the longer you hold down the mouse button, the further you jump) or try using a Flash spell.

Once back in the caverns, use the Recall item Mythran gave you to return to Argentrock Isle.

Go back to Windy Point and make your way to Stratos, saving on each rock.

Ask for the Breath of the Wind (she lowers you to your rock).

Cast Reveal, and you will see the Blackrock on a rock just to your northeast.

Use Aerial Servant to get the Blackrock, then use the Recall item to return to Mythran.

BLACKROCK PIECE FIVE

Ask Mythran about the Ether spell, and he'll tell you to read one of his books found on the upper level of his home.

Find and read the book ("Objective History of Pagan").

A new phrase is introduced into your speech: "I want to assemble the Pentagram."

Mythran will sell you the spell for 250 coins. You already have the regeants, namely the Blackrock.

When you return to the Castle, talk to Devon.

Get his key, go to the Castle's southwest corner, use the key and get the Tear of the Sea.

ETHEREAL PLANE: HYDROS

Once you have all five pieces of the Blackrock, click on the Ether spell book, then on the Tip of the Blackrock.

You will be transferred to the Ethereal Plane, where there are four doors.

The north is Hydros, the south Stratos.

The east is the Mountain King, the West is Pyros.

Go north to Hydros, then head west to several bridges.

When you come to a bridge that ends, with another end starting just north, jump to it.

Follow this up and around; you may encounter other bridges.

Check your position number by pressing Ctrl-V: when you reach 12164, 13905, 24, 25 you are near Hydros.

Go to 8692, 12912, 15, 45, and you will see a marble platform similar to the one you first encountered with Hydros.

Enter the center, and Hydros will appear.

Click on the Tear of the Sea, then on Hydros, who will disappear.

The Tear will glow blue, and you'll be teleported back to the Four Door Ethereal Plane.

ETHEREAL PLANE: STRATOS

Go south and, when you enter, go to the right side of the screen and jump only northeast to a nine-rock platform.

Ignore the rock paths with armor on them, which will collapse under you.

Save the game each time you make a successful jump.

You can safely walk and jump to a large rock consisting of nine rocks and a larger one in the north corner.

Several inviting targets lie scattered about, but ignore them and jump directly to the right side of the screen, location 14727, 5087, 184, 46.

After the second jump, your next target is north, to the upper right corner of the screen, then right again.

Jump over the small rock to the large one, then to the one with the overhang above it.

Be ready to click on the Breath of the Air, then on the vague lines above you, and once again you are transported back to the Four Door area.

ETHEREAL PLANE: PYROS

Go to Pyros, where arrive on a small island surrounded by lava (see note below before proceeding).

Jump southeast to a rock, then walk on lava, heading northeast, and jump north to the mainland.

Go all the way north and up some hills to a small temple.

Get the ten spheres from the jewelry box, then go south to the bridge.

Jump across the missing span and work your way north to a design with ten holes around it. Save the game.

Put the ten spheres into the ten holes, creating a stone north of you.

You should have no trouble jumping these, but save, as they disappear after you jump.

This leads you to a large circular pit, from which Pyros will emerge.

As quickly as possible, click on the Tongue and on Pyros, and you will be teleported back to the Ethereal Plane.

Note: You will be attacked by countless Demons in the preceding phase.

Take a lot of Banish Demon spells.

You will also be attacked by Seekers, many of which you can run away from.

Use Endure Heat, Rock Flesh, and Flame Armor if you have it.

At a side passage before going up to the ten-hole design, you can go over one more area.

Go north, and you will find a house with a lot of potions, which are probably worth the trouble.

Near the Temple to the north, stay around the edges of the land; the center portion has three of four weak spots, and you may fall through into lava.

ETHEREAL PLANE: MOUNTAIN KING

At the Mountain King, enter the door, and you will find yourself in a cavern.

As you go north, you will see three plateaus to jump up on.

Use the one nearest the left side of your screen.

Go north and west until you reach lava.

Then use Endure Heat and cross the lava to the west.

You will find a way up on the cliff ahead of you near the bottom of the ledge.

Do not go under the overhangs of the cliff, which conceal open lava.

Continue north and west to another pit.

Jump to the gravel to the north; use Grant Peace on any Skeletons or Ghosts.

Go to the end of the pit.

You can climb up at the extreme north end, then west and south to a very large room.

Save at once, then get the Heart of the Earth Blackrock ready.

The Mountain King will appear and summon several Golems to stop you.

Just click on the Blackrock, then on the Mountain King.

He will be destroyed, and you will be teleported to the Ethereal Plane.

ENDGAME

Four of the rocks are glowing.

Starting at number four on the large Pentagram in the middle of the room, put the rocks in as follows: Air, Fire, Water, Earth.

Double-click on Blackrock tip, then on yourself.

Put the Tip on the aphelion.

The Tip will glow and all will disappear.

A large Monolith will appear in the middle.

Watch it for a while: all the monsters you encountered are enclosed within.

Walk to it, and an animated sequence ends the quest.

ORBS & STUFF

Object	See this Section for Location	Also See Section(s)
Dagger	The Ceremonial Dagger	Location only
Invisibility Scroll	The Ceremonial Dagger	Location only
Monk's Hoods	Monk's Hoods	Location only
Wall spell	Monk's Hoods	Location only
Key of Scion	Heart of the Earth	This Way to Your Fate
Heart of the Earth	Heart of the Earth	This Way to Your Fate, Ethereal Plane: Mountain King
Slayer	The Slayer	Deceiver
Deceiver	Deceiver	Location only
Triangle Shield	This Way to Your Fate	Location only
Magic Scimitar	This Way to Your Fate	Location only
Quake Skull	Catacomb's Teleport	Location only
Protector	Monastery of Theurgy	Location only
Magic Helm	The Mage	Location only
Symbol	The Mage	Location only
Tongue of Flame	Malchir	Ethereal Plane: Pyros
Melchir's Staff	Malchir	Location only
Blackrock	Malchir, To the Caverns, Blackrock Piece Five	Ethereal Plane: Hydros
Tear of the Sea	Blackrock Piece Five	Ethereal Plane: Hydros

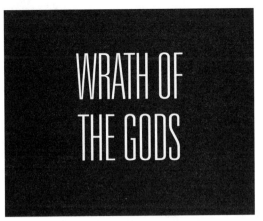

WRATH OF THE GODS

BY
FRED PHILIPP
AND CLANCY SHAFFER

T Y P E
*Graphic
Adventure*

S Y S T E M
*Macintosh &
IBM CD
(Required:
386/DX25+,
Windows 3.1,
4 MB RAM,
SVGA, mouse,
CD drive.
Recommended:
486DX, 8 MB
RAM, double-
speed CD
drive)*

C O M P A N Y
Luminaria

THE MORE YOU KNOW ABOUT GREEK MYTHS, THE BETTER IN *WRATH OF THE GODS*, BUT THE PROGRAM PROVIDES SUMMARIES THAT TELL EVERYTHING YOU NEED TO KNOW ABOUT THE PEOPLE, GODS, MONSTERS AND PLACES. RAISED BY A CENTAUR AFTER YOUR FATHER ATTEMPTS TO HAVE YOU SLAIN, YOU SET OUT TO COMPLETE A SERIES OF MINI-QUESTS BASED ON GREEK MYTHOLOGY. THEY INCLUDE SUCH EXPECTED CHALLENGES AS DEFEATING MEDUSA, THE CYCLOPS AND THE MINOTAUR. WHILE THE GRAPHICS, SVGA THROUGHOUT, ARE VERY GOOD, THE STORY OFTEN DRIFTS AND LEAVES YOU WONDERING WHAT TO DO NEXT. ANIMATION IS LIMITED TO MOUTH MOVEMENTS WHEN SOMEONE IS SPEAKING, BUT THE MONSTERS WERE CREATED WITH STOP-MOTION PHOTOGRAPHY, WHICH ENDOWS THEM WITH A CINEMATIC FLAIR. THE POINT AND QUEST INTERFACE MAKES IT EASY TO PLAY THIS GAME, THOUGH SOME ITEM ARE SO SMALL OR WELL-HIDDEN THAT IT IS NEARLY IMPOSSIBLE TO

GET YOUR HANDS ON THEM. PUZZLE-SOLVING REVOLVES AROUND FINDING OBJECTS, BUT THERE IS NO GENUINE COMBAT: IF YOU ARE CARRYING THE CORRECT ITEM, YOU AUTOMATICALLY WIN THE BATTLE. WITH PUZZLES THAT RANGE FROM EASY TO FRUSTRATING, *WRATH OF THE GODS* IS NO PUSHOVER, AND DESPITE A LOT OF MINOR DRAWBACKS, WILL SATISFY MOST SEEKERS OF ADVENTURE IN NEW DESTINATIONS.

THE SOLUTION

SOUTHWEST QUADRANT

SPEAK TO ANIMALS

Get gems and ring from Minotaur.

Exit west to Ruins.

Go west to Shrine, then to Pond and on to Rocks.

Click on keystone to cause an avalanche.

Pick up a rock and gem.

Return to Pond, then to Shrine.

Give gem to peddler for cake.

Put cake on altar, and you can now talk to animals.

HERA

Go east to Ruins, then south to River.

Help young woman cross the river, then return to river bank and help old woman cross.

The old woman is Hera, and she will give you a necklace.

JAIL

Go south to an encounter.

Get branch.

Talk to "couple of guys."

In jail, use bench six times on hole in wall to break through.

Go north to Pond.

Talk to rams.

TORCHBEARER

Return to Ruins, then go north to the Shepherd.

Use rock on boulder, then use branch on boulder to lift it.

Get sword and sandals.

Get the rock again.

Go north to Gloom.

Give a gem to Torchbearer.

Go east to Swamp.

Cross stones in the swamp to Hydra.

Return west (standing on east bank) and talk to Torchbearer.

HYDRA

The Torchbearer will join you.

Return to Hydra and lop off its heads with your sword.

The Torchbearer will cauterize wounds as you lop.

When the Hydra is dead, go east and talk to Eleusis.

Go west back to Gloom.

WAREHOUSE

Go north to Corinth, then west to Harvest and get Dragons Teeth.

Go north to Crossroads, west to Hades and enter.

Enter room with sledge hammers, select #2, then exit.

Exit Hades, go west to Chasm, push tree across, and go east to the Fork.

Continue east to Warehouse.

Use hammer on door, enter and get gem, vat of elixir and oars.

SEEDMEN

Return to Harvest and plant seeds (Dragons Teeth).

Fight Seedmen with sword.

Wait for zoom in and zoom out sequence.

Use elixir on yourself.

Throw rock among Seedmen to disorganize them.

Wait until Seedmen kill each other off.

RIVER STYX

Go north to the Crossroads, then north to Sciron.

Talk to Sciron, and you will be kicked off the ledge and find yourself in Hades, across the River Styx.

Walk along the river until you locate a Shade.

Talk to her, and she will give you a coin.

Return to the Boatman and use coin on yourself to cross river.

SCIRON

Return to Sciron and talk to him.

While you are kneeling, use hand icon on your foot to kick him off the ledge.

TARTARUS

Go south, east and north to Outside Castle.

Go east to a door outside Servants Quarters and enter.

Talk to King, sit in chair, and look at banners.

Pick banner #2 or #3.

The Queen will poison your wine, and you will die and arrive in Tartarus.

SHADE

Talk to Shade.

Use sledge hammer on any three objects in room to get a hint regarding King.

Exit to Hades and return to Castle.

KING

Talk, sit, and pick banner #1.

Give sword to King (he'll return it).

Show King your ring, and he'll give you a crown.

You will receive a message from your mother and a scroll.

Read scroll.

DIONE'S ROOM

Exit banquet hall through the other door.

Stand on patterns on floor in this order: pale green, dark green, gold, white.

Take tiara from the jewelry box in the wall panel.

Exit Castle and exit east to the Northwest Quadrant.

239

NORTHWEST QUADRANT

WATER NYMPH

Talk to Nymph, then jump into Pool.

Underwater, keep talking to Nymph until you surface.

Continue speaking with Nymph until she gives you a Helmet of Invisibility.

BEES

Go west to the hive and get wax.

Go east to the Pool and jump in to get rid of the bees.

ATHENA'S TEMPLE

Go west to Outside Temple and try to enter the Temple.

An offering from Hermes to is necessary to enter; you will return here much later.

EUROPA

Continue west to the Ruins, then west to Europa.

Arrange the blocks in alphabetical order according to the Greek alphabet (alpha, beta, gamma, delta) to open a panel and yield a gem.

Go west and note the Chimaera.

You'll eventually come back here and slay it, but not for a long while.

Getting juiced with Zeus.

GRAEAE

Return to Ruins, then go north.

Give peddler two gems for firewood, then take the carrot.

Go west and enter the Graeae Cave.

Grab the eyeball.

Offer to trade it back for the club.

Return the eyeball to the Graeae.

You will need the bow and arrows later.

NIGHT VISION

Return to peddler, then go east to Outside Hades, north to Cave and north to Hercules.

Talk to Hercules, then go north to Blackness.

Use carrot on yourself to see in the dark.

Follow path to Orpheus and take his lyre.

THESEUS

Continue on to Theseus and talk to him.

He is stuck to the rock.

Return to Hercules and tell him that you "need a hand."

He will follow you back to Theseus and free him.

CERBERUS

Continue past Theseus to Cerberus.

Use lyre to put Cerberus to sleep.

Continue past Cerberus to Treasury.

Use ATM and choose Pluto to get a gem.

Follow cave to Rock Slab, push it aside and exit cave.

Check map for your location.

JOUSTING

Return to Hercules, go to Elysian Fields, then head east to Jousting, where Perseus and Jason are jousting.

When you get a chance, talk to Perseus.

Pick up the staff that he dropped.

CLUBBING

Go west from Graeae, then north to Corynetes Arena.

Talk to Barker and challenge Periphetes to a fight.

Use club on him until you win the prize, a lump of lead.

Return to Graeae and get the bow and arrows.

SIREN

From Outside Hades, go east to Cyclops and try to get past him.

Continue going east until you reach the Clashing Rocks.

Take hardtack from barrel.

Talk to Sailor and climb on ship.

The ship will sail out of the harbor.

Click hardtack on gap in front of ship to lure bird to gap to spring trap there.

Put hand on tiller.

When you're through the gap, look at Siren.

Use wax on yourself to block ears.

Use tiller.

When sailor tries to talk to you, remove the wax.

You will shipwreck on the beach.

ON THE BEACH

Go east to Taverna and give one gem to the bartender.

Get bottle of wine.

Go east to King Aeetes.

Go north to the Golden Fleece.

Use hand on fleece, then fight Dragon.

You will die and arrive in Hades.

Talk to Tantalus, then grab the grapes for hints on getting the fleece.

Get gem.

Exit cave.

GOLDEN FLEECE

Return to the Golden Fleece.

Use hand on fleece, then use Lyre on yourself.

Use hand on Lyre and play the Siren's Song: 2, 1, 3, 4 strings.

Get the fleece.

CYCLOPS

Return to the billboard outside Hades Cave and go west to the Cyclops.

Give him the bottle of wine to put him to sleep.

You can now exit the Beach.

Go east to the Chariot Stop.

CHARIOT STOP

Enter and click on attendant, then click on slot machine.

If you have only one gem, you can win two by playing the machine: insert gem, pull handle, and take two gems.

For now, select your destination as Hesperides.

Give two gems to attendant for ticket.

Exit stop and climb onto Chariot.

Give ticket to chariot driver, and you'll take off for Hesperides.

————— NORTHEAST QUADRANT —————

ATLANTIS

Go west to Atlantis, then north to Atlas and talk.

You can return here later if you wish to play shooting gallery, but it is not necessary to complete the game.

Exit to Atlantis.

PAN

Go west to Pegasus Pasture, then west to Pan and talk.

Go west to the Landscape, then west to the Pillar (note the Fallen Pillar blocking your way).

Talk to the peddler.

Return to Pan and talk.

Go west to the Landscape then north to the Boat.

Put hand on boat, then put oars on boat.

Row to Island and pick up the string and reeds.

PAN PIPES

Return to Pan and use sword to carve reeds into pipes.

Add string to pipes, then give pipes to Pan.

Take pan pipes from Pan, and the Fallen Pillar is now removed.

CENTAUR

Go east to Pegasus Pasture, the north to Midas Touch and get Golden Apple.

Go north to Ruins and get gem.

Go west to Perseus, then west to Mt. Pelion Chariot Stop and north to the Centaur.

Talk to Centaur, then give him the apple.

Practice with bow (lead the targets by aiming ahead of them).

HERMES

Return to Midas Touch and go east to Olympus.

Climb up to the Balcony and go north to Hermes.

Walk carefully around the bed to get the Magic Sandals.

MEDUSA

Return to Perseus and go north to Near Medusa.

Walk east.

Medusa will appear and turn you to stone.

Hermes will appear, free you and give you a thigh bone.

Take the chariot back to Mycenae.

ATHENA

Go south to the Pool, then west to Outside Temple.

Use bone on Temple, then try to enter.

Go east to Pool and jump in to be purified.

Return to Temple and enter.

Walk forward and look at Athena on far left.

Put hand on Athena and talk to her, and she will give you a shield.

Return to Near Medusa.

MEDUSA'S HEAD

Give sword and shield to yourself.

Look at shield (mirror).

Walk east, and Medusa is automatically killed.

Wear the Helmet of Invisibility to become invisible.

Wear Hermes' Magic Sandals for stealth.

Exit to the west.

You are now carrying Medusa's Head.

GOLDEN GLOW

Go to Golden Glow, which is east of Perseus and east of Ruins.

Wear Hermes' sandals and click on Golden Glow to fly to it.

Get bridle and return to Road.

Go to Pegasus Pasture.

PEGASUS

Give yourself the staff, then give yourself the sword to sharpen it into a lance.

Give the lump of lead to yourself, then give yourself the lance to put lead on tip of lance.

Put bridle on Pegasus.

Climb on Pegasus to travel to the Chimaera.

CHIMAERA

Use lead-tipped lance on Chimaera to kill it.

Return to the Fallen Pillar in the Northeast Quadrant.

HERA

Go west and use pan pipes on Argus.

Go north to Caeneus.

Show Medusa's head to him, and he turns to stone.

Go north to Hera and talk.

You will find yourself on a beach with a ship offshore.

Swim aboard the ship.

Talk to King Minos and the Guard to travel to the Southeast Quadrant.

SOUTHEAST QUADRANT

CRETE (KNOSSOS)

Talk to Minos, then go west to axes.

Get axeheads and sticks.

Go north to the Well.

Pluck feather from bird.

Go north to the Maze.

Go east to Daedalus, talk and get candle.

Go west to the locked door.

Put hand on the door and talk.

The password is IO.

PRACTICE MAKES PERFECT

Go north to Bulls Leaping and practice jumping over the bull.

When you've got it down pat, return to the door and go west to the Throne.

ARIADNE

Get vase on the left and vase on the right.

Go east to Garden and talk to Ariadne.

Tell her "I need help please."

She will give you a clew.

Use vases on fountain to fill with water.

DIONE

Go east through door to Fire.

Use both vases to put out fire.

Get ember and go west to the Passageway.

Go west to Dione, talk to her and give her the tiara.

Return to Passageway.

WINGS

Go north to Terrace Vista.

Put sticks on ground, then put feather, wax and embers on ground, to make wings.

Get wings and use on yourself to fly to the sea in the northwest quadrant.

UNDERSEA

Return to Hera Temple and go north.

Talk to Minos and the bird to get the quest to retrieve ring.

Undersea, go north, north, east, north, east, east, south, south and east.

(Use "eye" to determine which direction is north.)

LABYRINTH

Talk to Mermaid and get the ring and crown.

Enter the Labyrinth and try swiping the torch.

Talk to Minos, then enter the Labyrinth.

If you wish, map the Labyrinth to escape; it's easier to use the Oracle twice to transport to the exit.

MINOTAUR

Put your hand on the Minotaur, then repeat to jump over.

Hit Minotaur on snout, then body, then snout again.

After defeating the Minotaur, exit to the west.

ZEUS

Use clew on anything in the room except the doorway.

You will travel to Mt. Olympus to meet with Zeus, who will shower you with accolades.

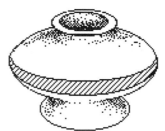

ORBS & STUFF

Object	See this Section for Location	Also See Section(s)
Gems	Speak to Animals	Graeae
Ring	Speak to Animals	King
Rock	Speak to Animals	Torchbearer
Gem	Speak to Animals	Torchbearer
Dragon's Teeth	Warehouse	Seedmen
Sledge Hammer	Warehouse	Shade
Gem	Warehouse	Graeae
Vat of Elixir	Warehouse	Seedmen
Oars	Warehouse	Pan
Coin	River Styx	Location only
Crown	King	Location only
Scroll	King	Location only
Helmet of Invisibility	Water Nymph	Medusa's Head
Wax	Bees	Siren
Gem	Europa	Graeae
Firewood	Graeae	Location only
Carrot	Graeae	Night Vision
Club	Graeae	Clubbing
Lyre	Night Vision	Cerberus
Gem	Cerberus	On the Beach
Staff	Jousting	Pegasus
Lump of Lead	Clubbing	Pegasus
Bow and Arrows	Clubbing	Centaur
Hardtack	Siren	Location only
Bottle of wine	On the Beach	Cyclops
Fleece	Golden Fleece	Location only
Gems	Chariot Stop	Location only
Ticket	Chariot Stop	Location only
String	Pan	Pan Pipes
Reeds	Pan	Pan Pipes
Pan Pipes	Pan	Hera
Golden Apple	Centaur	Location only
Gem	Centaur	Location only

249

Magic Sandals	Hermes	Medusa's Head
Medusa's Head	Medusa's Head	Hera
Bridle	Golden Glow	Pegasus
Thigh bone	Medusa	Location only
Shield	Athena	Medusa's Head
Axeheads	Crete	Location only
Sticks	Crete	Wings
Feather	Crete	Wings
Candle	Crete	Location only
Vases	Ariadne	Location only
Clew	Ariadne	Zeus
Ember	Dione	Wings
Wings	Wings	Location only
Ring	Labyrinth	Undersea
Crown	Labyrinth	Location only